The Maze Stone

Eileen Dunlop

The Maze Stone

Illustrated by Martin White

Oxford University Press 1982
Oxford New York Toronto Melbourne

Oxford University Press, Walton Street, Oxford OX2 6DP

London   Glasgow   New York   Toronto
Delhi   Bombay   Calcutta   Madras   Karachi
Nairobi   Dar es Salaam   Cape Town   Salisbury
Kuala Lumpur   Singapore   Hong Kong   Tokyo
Melbourne   Auckland

and associate companies in
Beirut   Berlin   Ibadan   Mexico City

© Eileen Dunlop 1982
First published 1982

All rights reserved. No part of this publication may be reproduced, stored in a retrieval system, or transmitted, in any form or by any means, electronic, mechanical, photocopying, recording, or otherwise, without the prior permission of Oxford University Press.

This book is sold subject to the condition that it shall not, by way of trade or otherwise, be lent, re-sold, hired or otherwise circulated without the publisher's prior consent in any form of binding or cover other than that in which it is published and without a similar condition, including this condition, being imposed on the subsequent purchaser.

British Library Cataloguing in Publication Data

Dunlop, Eileen
The maze stone.
I. Title
823'.914[J]   PZ7
ISBN 0-19-271458-9

Photoset in Great Britain by
Rowland Phototypesetting Ltd,
Bury St Edmunds, Suffolk
and printed by Biddles Ltd,
Guildford, Surrey

For my husband, Antony Kamm

The publisher acknowledges the financial assistance of the Scottish Arts Council in the publication of this volume.

The lines from 'Thank you for giving me the morning' are quoted by kind permission of Bosworth & Co. who have editions in print.

Contents

	1914	9
1.	The Hill	15
2.	Mr Lessing	23
3.	The Stone	29
4.	Morning Assembly	35
5.	The Invitation	45
6.	Supper on Sunday	54
7.	At the Ring of Trees	60
8.	Bad News for Hester	67
9.	A Public Inquiry	75
10.	Storms	84
11.	A Face from the Past	94
12.	Letters	101
13.	An Inward Music	108
14.	A Quarrel	115
15.	Spy	121
16.	At the Cowden Woods	129
17.	The Lordly Ones	136

1914

ON THE twenty-fourth of June, in the year 1914, a young man went into a house, and never came out again. His name was William Walter Gordon Maitland, aged twenty-two, of 14, Elliesland Street, Millhall, in the county of Lanarkshire, and one summer afternoon he vanished from the face of the earth. It was as simple, and as complicated, as that.

Such meagre details as the police were able to gather came mostly from his fiancée, Emily Wotherspoon, who had driven out with him after Sunday lunch, in her father's gig, to see the house, which was up for sale. They were to be married in August, and were looking for a home. Birkenshaw had been on the market for two years without finding a purchaser, and the asking price had been several times reduced. With their savings – William was a bank clerk and Emily a school teacher – and some help from Emily's farmer father, they reckoned they could afford to buy the place. They had set off in high spirits; often, afterwards, the Wotherspoons would remark how cheerful William had been that day, as if, in some way, that were a comfort to them now.

'Tell me everything that happened,' the Police Inspector said, with kindly pity for the bewildered girl. 'Take your time, lass, and just let me hear it as it comes into your mind. Start with the journey out.'

So Emily told him, trying hard to keep to the facts which she vaguely supposed a policeman would want to hear, but unable to help confusing these with other memories, the sun beating on her back as they drove along, the slow whirring of insects in the steep, flower-stippled banks on either side of the road, the small grey spurts of dust under the horse's hoofs, William's strong brown hands twined lightly in the reins. In the beginning, it had been such a lovely day.

The Inspector listened patiently, his pencil poised above his notebook.

'So you came to the house,' he said.

Emily repeated, 'So we came to the house.'

'Did you see anyone?'

'No. Oh no, not a soul.' She paused thoughtfully, then went on. 'It was quite deserted. The gate was open. Yes. Its hinges were broken, I think. There was honeysuckle in the hedge. The garden was terribly overgrown – William said, wasn't it a good thing we both liked gardening, because it was going to take ages to put it in order. There was moss on the steps, too, and grass and stonecrop growing in the cracks in the stone. Not that we'd have minded that sort of thing. It was the inside we didn't like.'

Emily shivered, although it was too warm in the farm kitchen, where pots were simmering constantly on the wide iron range.

'You didn't like the inside of the house,' the Inspector prompted. 'Why was that, my dear?'

'Well, it was so dark, you see, and icy cold. Of course, we knew that nobody had lived in it for years and years, not since old Miss Russell died when I was just a little girl. We didn't expect it to be clean, or pretty, or anything like that, only – oh, it's hard to describe what was wrong with it. It wasn't just that the paint was peeling, and the paper falling off the walls where the damp patches were – or even that the windows at the back looked straight out on to that hill they call Bieldlaw, which is such a queer place, don't you think? I can't explain. It just didn't feel right.'

Emily sat staring in front of her, twisting her engagement ring round and round on her finger. It had pearls in it, which her mother said were unlucky. Pearls were for tears. The Inspector, who was professionally more concerned with facts than with feelings, watched her, and dismissed her words as those of someone who, in distress, imagines more than was really true at the time. That the young man's disappearance seemed mysterious, he agreed, but he was a policeman, trained to believe that there was a rational explanation for everything, and that vague talk of places not feeling right should be discounted as having nothing to do with evidence. Yet even as he responded in this proper, policemanly way, he remembered inconveniently that hill behind Birkenshaw, the stories his granny used to tell about it, and how as a small boy he would come home the long way by the road, rather than cross its flank in the gloaming. Bieldlaw, its name was on the maps, but the old folk called it Elvanknowe . . . He wrote the words, 'Queer place', on his notebook, frowned, and crossed them out again.

'Miss Wotherspoon,' he said gently, 'I want you to describe to me, very carefully, what happened next. Am I right in thinking that you both came out of the house, and that Mr Maitland then went back in?'

Emily made an effort, and concentrated her thoughts. It would have been easier if there had not been an echo, strangely like music, resounding inside her head, but she did her best.

'Yes,' she said slowly. 'We were both disappointed. We neither of us said so, but I was, and I could sense how William was feeling. In fact, he was more upset than I was, all jumpy and on edge. He said, "No point in waiting about here. Let's get out in the sunshine again." He loved the sun, couldn't get enough of it, ever. So we came out. It was hotter than ever, and we could hear thunder far away. William said, all hasty, "Better get back, there's a storm brewing," and we walked back down the path to where we had left the gig. William helped me in, and I thought he was going to climb up too, but then he said, "Blast. I've left my hat in the kitchen. You wait here, Emmy – it won't take a minute to fetch it." He put his foot on the step, jumped up and kissed me, then he ran back up the path to the house.'

'You saw him go in?'

'Yes.' She was quite definite about it. 'I watched him unlock the door, and I saw him go in.'

And really, the Inspector reflected later, there was little more that the poor girl could usefully tell. She had waited she could not say how long, ten minutes perhaps, while the bees droned in the honeysuckle, and the house lay like a dark blot on the shimmering summer fields. Then she began to think that William was long in coming, but she had not worried; he was, she supposed, looking over the house again, perhaps thinking of ways to make it, unpromising as it was, into the home they had imagined it would be. William, Emily said with innocent pride, was so clever with his hands. Only when she had waited as long again, and the heat was making her head ache, did she climb down from the gig, and go to fetch him. But the door was locked, and no amount of hammering and calling and knocking on the cobweb-shrouded windows had brought the young man forth.

Then a terrible, nightmare panic had seized Emily by the throat. Forgetting the horse, standing patient and motionless at the gate, she had set off running across the fields to the nearest farm, more than half a mile distant. Hampered by her narrow skirt and slender, pointed shoes, she could not move quickly, and meantime the storm which had begun as a small, unheeded smudge on the western horizon erupted across the sky, wiping out the sun and bringing rain, first in splashes, then in a downpour of stinging spears. Thunder followed lightning flash, and by the time that Emily arrived at the farm, her pink cotton dress was smeared with mud from collar to hem, she had lost her hat, and her shoes were in tatters. She was barely able to gasp out her story to the farmer's wife before sinking down exhausted on the threshold.

The farmer's wife, though kindly, could not share Emily's alarm. She took her in, and dried her, and pacified her, but not until the rain had stopped would she allow her son, and one of the farm servants, to go out across the fields to Birkenshaw. The front door was locked, but yielded to a well-placed kick; the key was in the lock on the inside of the door, and the house was empty. It was noted, not by the farm folk, but by the Police, who were called later that evening, when William had failed to return either to the Wotherspoon farm or to his lodgings in Millhall, that the back door was bolted both inside and out, with bolts that had not been disturbed for many years. The windows, too, were locked fast, with no rents in their soft cobweb-curtains to suggest that anyone had tried to get out that way. There were no signs of violence. William Maitland's brown bowler hat was on the stained wooden draining-board beside the dried-up kitchen sink, but William Maitland was never seen again.

The Police made careful enquiries, and the local people indulged for a while in speculation, most of it macabre. But no bodily trace of the young man was ever found. Nor much other trace, indeed. William Maitland had come to work in Millhall three years previously, from Glasgow; even Emily was vague about his background, other than that he was an orphan, but had an aunt, she thought, living over Tinto way. William, she said, had never seemed to want to talk about his life before they met. Attempts to discover the aunt failed, and a search of William's rooms in Elliesland Street disclosed no letters, no address book, no private papers of any kind. More oddly still, when the Police applied to Register House, in Edinburgh, for a copy of his birth certificate, it was discovered that, unlawfully, the event had never been recorded.

Then the War came, and with it the disappearance of so many young men that William's, though stranger, came to seem less dramatic. The following year, the Police Inspector who had questioned Emily was killed, fighting against the Germans at Ypres, and five years after that, Emily married a farmer from neighbouring Midlothian, moving without regret from Hartslawhead. William Maitland's became a name in a Police file, never officially closed, but never actually opened; time went by and, motherless, fatherless and friendless as he was, he was forgotten.

The house of Birkenshaw, of course, was doomed. No one would live there after the mysterious death – for it could be called nothing else – of young Mr Maitland, that nice lad from the Bank. Long after William's name had passed into silence, the house retained its bad reputation. Black and brooding and empty, it became a prey to thieves, and later to vandals, till the lead was gone from its roof, the glass from its windows, the old Dutch tiles from its hearths, while wind and rain blew eerily in at doors half off their hinges. Fifty years passed, then sixty; it was engulfed, with its wildly flourishing garden, in the creeping urban sprawl of the twentieth century, and eventually pulled down.

Its fall stirred faint memories. Down at the new Eventide Home, there were some ancient mutterings about foul play, and bones under the floorboards – only nobody could remember whose bones they were likely to be.

They pulled down the house, and they dug up the garden, but they left the hedge with the honeysuckle, to divide a new housing development from the main road. Emily Wotherspoon would not have approved of that. She was to hate the scent of honeysuckle till the day she died.

1. The Hill

NEARLY SEVENTY years on, there are still June days in Hartslawhead like the one on which William and Emily took their last ride together, only now it is concrete pavement which returns the sun's white stare, not the hazy, pale summer fields. It was seven o'clock in the evening of such a day, Sunday the second, to be precise, and all down Birkenshaw Gardens families were having supper in kitchens with wide open windows and doors. There had not been a breath of wind since morning.

The Mowbrays were sitting around their kitchen table, silent and exhausted by the heat. Their supper had been eaten, but no one could summon the energy to start washing up. Dr Mowbray was reading the local newspaper, which had made its weekly appearance the previous day. His wife, who had cleared herself a space among the plates and coffee cups, was correcting Latin ink exercises; she had been pushing this task away from her all week-end, and now it was urgent. Hester was languidly removing Saturday night's nail varnish from her finger-nails. She was not really allowed to do this sort of thing in the kitchen, but she had calculated, correctly, that her mother would be too weary to make a fuss. Fanny, who never varnished her finger-nails, was sitting perfectly still, opposite the open door, staring intently into the past. The present and the future alike were of no interest to her at all.

For a while, the silence was broken only by the rustle of paper, and Mrs Mowbray's tongue clicking impatiently over some silly error, but then suddenly Dr Mowbray looked up with an unaccustomed frown between his eyebrows; normally he was the most even-tempered of men.

'Well, well,' he said. 'Well, well. There's going to be trouble about this.'

'Trouble about what?' Mrs Mowbray paused with her red biro suspended above a page, giving him approximately half her attention.

Hester pricked up her ears. 'What's up now, Stuart?' she demanded cheerfully.

'It's this report,' said Dr Mowbray uneasily, jabbing at the newsprint with a long forefinger. 'It hardly seems credible. It appears that someone from the north of England wants to open up a quarry on Bieldlaw, and our enlightened District Council is all in favour of the project. Pious utterances from the Convener about local unemployment and unexploited resources – the usual sort of codswallop. Alison, you're not listening.'

'I *am* listening.' Mrs Mowbray had put down her pen, and was staring at him over her spectacles in a mixture of disbelief and horror.

'Oh, you can't believe a single word you read in the "Squeak",' put in Hester comfortingly.

This was the general opinion of those who bought the *Millhall and District Courier* every Saturday; nonetheless, it was looked forward to, and read avidly.

'This sounds likely enough, unfortunately,' said Dr Mowbray ruefully. 'If you know the Council, it has a horrible ring of truth about it. Bieldlaw is the only place around here they haven't contrived to ruin already.'

Mrs Mowbray erupted into speech. 'Stuart, they can't. They just can't. Bieldlaw's practically on our doorstep. A quarry, for heaven's sake! Just think of the mess – not to mention the noise, the stone-blasting, and lorries thundering up and down. When you think what we had to pay for this place, and that we'd never be able to sell it –'

'All right, steady on, love,' interrupted her husband soothingly. 'As Hester says, the "Squeak" 's awfully good at getting things wrong, and even if this time the story is true, there are various things that can be done to oppose it – to stop it, if we go about things the right way. I think I'll just step over to Rory Simpson's for a few minutes – he's the Chairman of that Civic Amenities Council they started last year – and ask what thoughts he has on the subject. It wouldn't do any harm to have a few plans made in advance, just in case we do have a fight on our hands.' He heaved himself on to his feet, tossed the newspaper aside, and added, 'If there should be a call for me, send Fanny over to Rory's. You'll come for me, won't you, Fan?'

Fanny came slowly back from the place where her mind had been, looked up at her father, and said, 'Sorry. What?'

'You'll come to fetch me from Mr Simpson's, if there's a call for me?'

'Yes, of course, Dad.'

'Right. Then I'll be off.'

Dr Mowbray went out by the back door, and passed the window, his curly head dark against the sunlit turf of Bieldlaw, which filled the whole rectangle of glass. Hester got up too, carefully screwing the cap on to her bottle of nail varnish remover.

'I'm going up to Molly's,' she said to her mother. 'We're going to play records, and make some posters for the school Debating Society. I'm telling you before you ask, which proves what a good, kind, thoughtful daughter I am, not like the ones you see in the plays on the telly. I shan't be late.'

Mrs Mowbray laughed, but she said firmly, 'Ten o'clock, please. I know what your notion of late and early is, and it's a school day tomorrow. Remember, Hester.'

Hester sighed. 'What a life. Cheers, Fanny,' she said, and left.

Mrs Mowbray put a mark out of ten in the margin of the last exercise book, slapped it shut, took off her spectacles and looked at Fanny.

'And what are you going to do tonight, little one?' she asked gently.

'I'll help you wash up,' Fanny said. 'Then I think I'll go up on the hill for a little while. There are rabbits up there, and if you keep still, they come quite close to you, nibbling at the grass.' She caught Mrs Mowbray's eye, and went on hastily, 'I'm all right, Alison, honestly I am. Don't worry about me, please.'

Mrs Mowbray stood up and began to collect the plates, and stack them beside the sink.

'Go up on the hill, if that's what you want to do, love,' she said. 'I can quite easily manage the washing up on my own tonight. But don't stay out too long. These summer nights are chilly, and I don't want you catching cold.'

Fanny grabbed her scarlet jersey, which was hanging over the back of her chair, and wriggled into it. She was almost through the door when she stopped, and turned round.

'I forgot. What about Dad?' she said.

'I'll fetch him, if need be.'

'Well, thanks, Alison. I'll see you later.'

With her hands thrust into the pockets of her denim jeans, Fanny walked down the narrow strip of garden behind the house. There was a fence, then a beaten footpath, then the hillside, a swift green sweep which levelled out half-way up on to a wide, grassy platform, then rose again towards a sharply conical peak, crowned with a frill of small, windcrippled trees. It was a peculiar hill, sinister in certain moods of weather, rearing its head incongruously above the newtown brick-and-concrete maze of Millhall and Hartslawhead which occupied more than half of its perimeter. It had been saved from the fate of every other green place in the district only because it was unsuitable as building land. Fanny climbed over the fence, crossed the path, and began to climb the hill. The sun, coming down the sky but not yet near its setting, sent beams slanting down the corridor between the walls of the houses and the lower slope; the turf was warm and astir with insects living a hectic evening life, in and out of the clover and the rough blades of grass.

Fanny went up slowly. She was, her father and Dr

Malcolm considered, quite recovered from the illness which had kept her in bed for weeks in the winter, but she could not yet do strenuous things quickly. Sometimes this could be very frustrating, but now it did not matter; she was not in a hurry, and it was pleasant to sit down every now and then on the dry, springy grass, and feel the sun, which had been so cruelly hot at midday, gently warming her back. Fanny did not, as Mrs Mowbray knew perfectly well, come up on the hill to look for rabbits, although there were rabbits, further up. She came up to be alone in the only place which reminded her even faintly, by its sounds, feels and smells, of the world she knew and hungered for constantly, finding no pleasure in anything that her new world had to offer. Which was terrible, for the old ways were gone for ever. Even if she could go back, nothing would be the same.

Until six months ago, Fanny had not lived with her father and stepmother in their new detached villa in Birkenshaw Gardens, Hartslawhead. She had lived, as she always had, ever since her mother had been killed in a road accident when Fanny was three, with her grandmother, in an old sandstone house behind a high wall, on the edge of a small village in Roxburghshire, near the English Border. The village was scarcely more than a scatter of cottages on either side of a winding country road, but it had an Inn, and in the front room of one of the cottages a shop, which was also the Post Office. There was a smithy, still in use, and a telephone kiosk, and a red Victorian letter-box set into the churchyard wall. Opposite Fanny's grandmother's house, a little weathered grey church stood on a rise; it had no gloomy stained glass, but clear window panes, so that you could sit in the pew on a Sunday morning, with the Minister's voice droning pleasantly in your ears, watching the play of sun and shadow on the old grey gravestones, and amuse yourself naming the birds, and the wild flowers in the grass. Beyond the church was the manse, and beyond the manse the road rose suddenly into the hills, blue and green and purple and white by turns as the seasons passed over them. Fanny had gone to school on the country bus each day, and had enjoyed her lessons, but her real life had been in her grandmother's house, reading books and working in the herb garden, learning how to make the natural medicines from herbs which people liked so much that they sent orders for them from all over the world.

And then, one morning, it was all over. It was in December, and dark, and her grandmother had failed to call Fanny for school. Fanny had overslept, and waking with the dawn, had run in her nightdress to her grandmother's room, to wake her too.

'Granny! Wake up! It's twenty to nine . . .'

They usually rose before seven. She had stood there in her bare feet, gently shaking the thin old body under the quilt, but in vain. Her grandmother had died, all unexpectedly, in her sleep. That very day her father had come, and brought her, stunned and disbelieving, to live at Hartslawhead.

Fanny was reliving this experience – she was always reliving it, which was why she was so unhappy – as she gained the level platform half-way up Bieldlaw, and made her way along the ridge to the standing stones, two great upright boulders which were all that remained, people said, of a circle that had stood there in ancient times. Under one of these stones there was a hollowed, private place where you could sit comfortably against the rain-smoothed rock, with your back to the view. It was a magnificent view, which encompassed smoke-coloured mountains, shining lochs and a silver line of sea, but there were also slag heaps, and factory chimneys, and columns of spiky pylons in it, which Fanny hated. She preferred to turn away, and be alone with the burden of her sorrow, which she made not the least effort to discard. She climbed down into the hollow, and made herself comfortable, then she began to torture herself, recalling her little attic bedroom at Yesterlee, and the garden, and her grandmother's spare, upright figure coming down the sward with the watering-cans. Fanny could not have explained to anyone how she felt, but it was as if she was afraid to stop remembering her grandmother for even a moment, in case she should suddenly find that she could not remember her at all.

It never occurred to her that she was perhaps being unfair to her father and Alison and Hester, who had been so kind to her. She had always been fond of her father, although she had never lived with him, and she liked Alison, who had tried hard to make her feel at home, and who had nursed her so kindly when, in January, she had fallen ill with pleurisy, and had had to stay in bed for six weeks. And it was Hester, a year older than herself, who had found her that winter day after school, leaning against the wall of the cycle shed, too ill to ride her bicycle home, Hester who had helped her back to the cloakroom, and fetched a teacher to take her home by car. All the time she had been in bed, too, Hester had come to see her every day, and brought her books, and told her the school news in a friendly, joky fashion. Hester would have been a good friend to her, Fanny knew, if only she had not been too miserable to respond. Eventually, Hester had stopped trying. She went on being nice to Fanny in a casual way, but she sought the company of her own friends at school, and was always very busy with her studies, and hockey, and her parts in the school Dramatic Society. Hester was bright and popular, with fashionably cut dark hair, and a way of wearing her school uniform as if it were an outfit from a Paris salon. Fanny thought she always looked very nice, and would have been astonished to know that Hester secretly envied her her dark blue eyes and wildly curling golden hair.

As Fanny sat under the rock, the sun dipped out of sight, making the hill's edge sharp against a luminous silver glow. She was not aware of time passing, or even of the sharp, sudden chill which often mars the still, clear beauty of a northern summer night. Twilight came, and she might have sat on there till Alison, none too pleased, came up to fetch her, had not her attention been caught by an unaccustomed movement on the hillside above. She seldom met anyone on Bieldlaw, and never at night; that was its charm for her. Now she looked up, and saw a man emerge from the trees on the crown of the hill. Far up, and far away, he stood motionless for a moment, a thin, dark silhouette upon the grass. Then he began to descend swiftly, in a slithering scramble over the first steep incline, but as he came to the gentler slope, with loping, graceful steps. As he came nearer, Fanny saw that he was quite young, with longish red hair, and the customary young man's uniform of denim jeans and matching jacket. He was ordinary; one saw dozens of people like him in the street every day. Certainly there was nothing about him to explain the wave of terror that now washed coldly over Fanny; she could not have been more afraid if he had been coming at her with a knife. It was true that he had appeared unexpectedly, but why on earth should the sight of a stranger, out like yourself for an evening ramble, make you cower back into the shelter of the standing stone, fearful of being seen, make you tremble all over, leave your palms wet and your teeth chattering, and your heart beating like a drum? Especially when he didn't even glance in your direction, but veered off to the right a hundred yards from the stones, disappearing over the ridge in the direction of the Lanark Road? It was absurd, and Fanny knew it was absurd; even as she herself scrambled back along the ridge, and plunged downhill towards home, she remembered overhearing her father remarking to Alison, some time before, that Fanny's nerves were in a bad state. She had been indignant at that time, as no one cares for criticism of their nerves, but now, as she pushed open the back door, and felt herself relaxing in the humdrum surroundings of a modern kitchen, she found herself wondering bleakly whether perhaps he was right, after all.

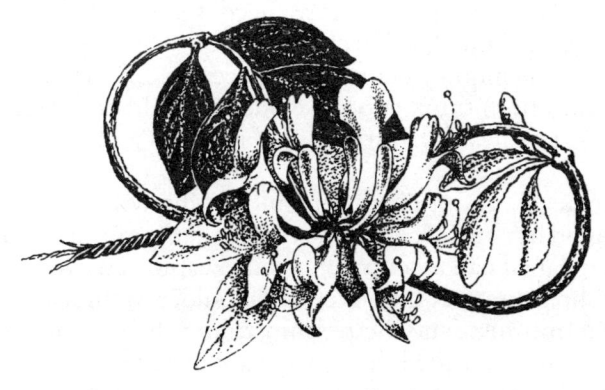

2. Mr Lessing

No CALL had come for Dr Mowbray, and he had spent the evening at Rory Simpson's, relaxing with a glass of beer in Rory's back garden, and indulging in the pleasant pastime known as 'putting the world to rights'. They had discussed the variable fortunes of the local Cricket Club, compared notes on how to eliminate moss and clover from one's lawn, asked politely how each other's children – Rory had five – were getting on at school, and only late in the evening got down to considering the report in the *Courier*, and what they would do if – which Heaven forbid – it should prove to have foundation.

Dr Mowbray reported to his family over breakfast next morning.

'We reckon the whole place would be up in arms,' he said. 'Hartslawhead is a residential district, and a quarry wouldn't offer much employment to any of the folk who live round here. Besides, it's the only bit of green land we have left, and Rory has a notion that when the plans for the public park were scrapped by the Council a few years back, one of their excuses was that Bieldlaw offered the same facilities as a park. A matter of opinion, of course, but a handy piece of ammunition if we need it. Anyway, if we all stick together and object in concert, there'd have to be some sort of public inquiry before the project got off the ground. Rory and I both think enough evidence could be presented on our side – health hazard, loss of amenity and so on – to stop it.'

He paused, and looked hopefully at his wife, who was putting on her lipstick at the stove, using the polished facing above the grill pan as a mirror, while keeping an eye on the toast. She glanced at him over her shoulder, dubiously. He was the optimist, she the pessimist, and their being-right scores, as Hester called them, were about even.

'Well, I hope so, Stuart,' she said, turning back to snatch two pieces of toast from the flames. 'I can think of nothing more ghastly than a quarry on Bieldlaw. Honestly, I can think of nothing more ghastly.'

'I must admit I can't either,' replied Dr Mowbray, his optimism faltering just a trifle. 'However, I have to be off. I've an early surgery at Millhall this morning. Have a nice day, girls.'

Fanny and Hester left the house together, and made their way down Birkenshaw Gardens to the main road, where the bus stop grew incongruously out of the hedge. Even so early in the morning, the scent of honeysuckle was overpowering, and Fanny sniffed it appreciatively, while her eye condemned the tatter of potato crisps bags and cigarette packets which clung about the dusty roots. Hester was in a bubble of good spirits, and for want of Molly, who went to school by car, she chatted to Fanny.

'We're having the new English teacher today,' she said. 'His name is Mr Lessing. I'm looking forward to it. He's going to take our class for Drama – we're to read *The Merchant of Venice* with him. I've got Mother's copy, with lots of notes written in, so that I can ask clever questions and impress him.'

Fanny, who was as usual doing her Maths homework in the bus queue, looked up from the quadratic equations and said, 'Whatever do you want to impress him for?' in an astonished tone of voice.

'Listen,' said Hester. 'He used to be an actor, a proper one, in London, in the West End. So if I impress him favourably, he may be able to help me in my career, later on. See? And in the meantime, he should be a change from all these other drearies in the English Department.'

'Yes. You're lucky,' agreed Fanny gloomily. 'I'm stuck with the awful Mole, till the end of term at least. She's got this thing about Matthew Arnold, and she keeps making remarks about my jersey, as if it was any business of hers.'

Hester grinned. Fanny's jersey was a talking point in the school, where the wearing of uniform was encouraged, though not altogether enforced. Fanny had, from the beginning, refused to wear the white blouse and blue tie which the other girls wore under their blue blazers; under the grey blazer of her last school she wore a red polo-necked jersey, and when the Lady Adviser, or Miss Mole, or anyone else tried to persuade her to be like the others, she smiled vaguely, putting on what Hester called her daffy look, and paid no attention whatsoever. Hester rather admired this quiet insubordination, although she was herself too conventional to copy it.

After a long wait, the bus came.

The High School at Millhall was a hideous cuboid erection of orange brick and plate glass, set down in acres of dusty green playing-field. Long before the building was finished, it had become obvious that it was far too small for the burgeoning teenage population of the district, and the school yard had immediately disappeared under an unattractive litter of prefabricated huts. Here the younger pupils, like Fanny, had most of their classes, sprinting to and from the main building for gym and music and lunch. Hester had left the huts when she reached Fourth Year, and attained certain privileges, such as being allowed to keep herself warm and dry all day. So she and Fanny rarely saw each other during school hours; when they got off the bus Fanny, who regularly skipped Morning Assembly, went off to hut 3A to finish her Maths, while Hester proceeded to the Fourth Year cloakroom, where she met up with Molly and her other friends.

There was a great deal of interest in the new English teacher, especially among the girls. Many, indeed most, of the High School staff were young, but none was as exciting as an actor from London. When Assembly was over, and the class gathered in the form room overlooking the school kitchen and the rugby field, there was a pleasurable rustle of anticipation through the usual frantic searching for books, borrowing and sharpening of pencils, and, on the boys' side, discussion of the Saturday football results. Now that they were in Fourth Year, and everything they did was examinable, there was less skylarking in class than of yore; still, a new teacher might afford a little fun. The noise broke off suddenly as the door opened, and Mr Lessing came in.

He was a tall, thin young man with floppy red hair and a flushed, suntanned face. His eyes, as he glanced around the room, were dark and sharply bright. He put his books on the table, took off his leather jacket, and slung it over the back of the teacher's chair with one long brown hand. He was wearing corduroy trousers and a black open-necked shirt, and he had a large silver medallion on a chain round his neck. He was rather less flamboyant than most of the teachers under thirty in the school, but, Hester thought, a thousand times more attractive. She was determined to find him marvellous. There was a watchful silence while the class summed him up; in ten minutes, perhaps, one of the boys might try a little prank, just to test the ground. But not yet.

'Open the windows, you at the back,' he said, suddenly and sharply. 'And the rest of you, open your books at page ten. You've all heard of Shakespeare, I suppose. This is one of his comedies, which isn't to say it's a laugh from start to finish. Now, keep the place. Act I, Scene I, A Street in Venice. Enter Antonio . . .' He began to read, in a deep, chiming voice such as Hester never recollected having heard before. It seemed to have a similar effect on other people, including all those who regarded Shakespeare as a Waste of Time, for the testing prank never happened, and the bell rang at ten o'clock without Hester's having had much chance to be impressive.

At break, however, in the dining-room, something delightful happened. When Hester and Molly had collected their coffee, and Molly the doughnut without which she said she could never get through the morning, and had settled themselves where they could watch Mr Lessing drinking his orange juice at the staff table, they were dumbfounded to see him bypass the staff corner of the vast dining-room, and stroll across to where they were sitting.

'Hello,' he said. 'You were in my class this morning, weren't you? Do you mind if I join you?'

Hester was temporarily bereft of speech, but Molly, who was a friendly, cheerful little robin of a girl, recovered quickly from her surprise and said, 'Please do. Although it isn't usual. There are tablecloths, if you sit with the teachers.'

Mr Lessing laughed, and sat down, stowing his jacket and folders under his chair.

'I can live without tablecloths, if the company's good,' he said. 'What are your names?'

'I'm Molly Wilson,' said Molly, 'and this is Hester Field. Do you think you're going to like Millhall, Mr Lessing? It'll be a change from the West End of London.'

'Oh, I haven't always been in London,' he replied. 'I've been around a lot. I don't expect I'll find Millhall worse than any other place. Do you like it?'

'Don't know,' replied Molly. 'I never really notice. It rains a lot.'

At this point, Hester found her tongue.

'Mr Lessing,' she said eagerly, 'have you really played in the West End? It must have been terribly exciting. What plays were you in?'

'*Hedda Gabler* at the Haymarket,' he said, turning his head towards her, 'and two plays at the National – *Pericles* and *The Importance of Being Earnest*.'

'The National,' breathed Hester. 'Gosh.'

'Do you have a special name for the stage?' enquired Molly. 'Or is it Lessing there too?'

'Nimmo Lessing, at your service,' he replied, grinning at

her. Hester thought he looked like the Pied Piper, with his bright brown eyes and curly, laughing mouth, which, unfortunately, was encouraging Molly to speak her mind.

'Nimmo Lessing?' she screeched happily. 'That's a scream. But is it your real name?'

'I've had others.'

'For the stage, I suppose you mean,' Molly said. 'Well, Nimmo Lessing's great, if you ask me. It's so daft, no one would be likely to forget it.'

'Molly!' cried Hester, scandalised.

Mr Lessing smiled at her, and shook his head.

'It's all right,' he said. 'I'm not offended. It's true enough, in a way. There's a lot in a name, on the stage. Now yours would be a good one, if I may say so.'

Hester felt a momentary pang of relief that she had not yielded to a temptation she sometimes experienced, to change her name from Field to Mowbray. She smiled back at him, but just managed to avoid showing how much his remark delighted her. How odd, she thought, that he should have made it, not knowing that to be an actress was her dearest wish.

Just then, the bell rang for the end of break, and there was a mass exodus from the dining-room. Molly had to take her doughnut with her, having forgotten to eat it in the novel situation of having coffee with a teacher. Mr Lessing got up, gulped down his orange juice, and retrieved his belongings from under his chair.

'I'll see you again – Wednesday, isn't it?' he said. 'Be good till then.'

And they went their separate ways.

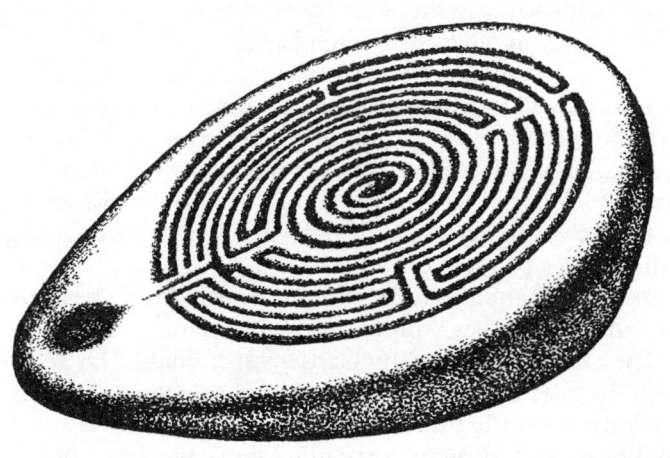

3. The Stone

THAT EVENING after school, while Hester was in her room reading Shakespeare, Fanny helped her father in the garden. By Fanny's standards, and indeed by Dr Mowbray's, the strip of land to the rear of their brashly modern house scarcely deserved the name of garden; however, it was better than nothing, and sometimes Fanny was almost happy there, hoeing and watering and pricking out seedlings in the tiny greenhouse outside the back door. Until she remembered the old walled garden at Yesterlee, that is, with its herbaceous borders and fine old trees. Then misery came sweeping back, and the colour drained out of everything.

One thing did fascinate her, however, and her father no less, and that was the tendency in their garden for flowers to appear which they had never planted. In spring, frail cream daffodils had sprung up, followed later in the year by random eruptions of old-fashioned flowers, stocks and delphiniums, pinks and lupins, and, along the margin of the footpath between the garden and the hill, a wild ramble of thin, sweetly scented roses. Dr Mowbray explained to

Fanny that formerly theirs had been part of a larger garden, belonging to an old house called Birkenshaw.

'It was a shocking old place,' he told her, 'ramshackle beyond belief. It was still standing when I came to these parts in 1967, but they must have pulled it down shortly afterwards. The garden was a wilderness – hadn't been touched for decades, I should think. But you could see that it had once been very beautiful. That's where these flowers come from – you just can't keep flowers down.'

Fanny thought about this for a moment, then she asked, 'Are all these houses built in that old garden?'

'The ones in Birkenshaw Gardens are,' replied Dr Mowbray. 'In fact, when we bought ours, I remember getting a brochure from the builder which said that stones from the old house had been incorporated into the new ones. I suppose in ours they used them for the stone fireplace in the sitting-room. It's rather nice, don't you think?'

'It's all right,' said Fanny unenthusiastically.

There had been a Robert Adam fireplace in the drawing-room at Yesterlee.

Today, wearing old jeans, and with the sleeves of her red jersey rolled up to keep them clean, Fanny was helping her father to weed the vegetable plot. Squatting down with bent knees, she pulled up groundsel and pale willow-herb and forget-me-not, which grew just as keenly as cabbages in the rich soil, and tossed them into the dustbin lid, which provided a handy carrying tray. Though the sky was clear, the garden was mostly in shadow, and a light breeze which had not blown yesterday ruffled Fanny's hair. It was not so oppressively hot.

Fanny was glad of the slight change in the weather. It had not been a pleasant day. She had risen aching and weary after a hot, restless night, when she had got herself hopelessly tangled in the bedclothes, and drifted from taut sleeplessness through periods of light, uneasy sleep. Then she had dreamed of standing stones the height of church towers, which rocked and teetered and toppled before she could escape from their shadow, and of being pursued along the tops of precipices by a nameless, faceless man. Then there had been school, and the kind of day when everything goes awry. The Maths exercise she had done on the bus had been wrong from start to finish, she had lost her gym shoes, then her lunch ticket, and her dullness and lack of concentration had been remarked upon at practically every class she had attended. Now it was nice to be home, and out in the fresh air, which had blown away her headache for the first time since morning.

She had not yet got over her fright of the night before, however. She worked with her back to the hill, and even when she had to face it, coming back from the compost heap with the empty lid, she avoided lifting her eyes to the tree-ring high above, where last night the stranger had made his appearance. She knew that she was behaving ridiculously, and was intensely irritated by her own silliness, but there seemed nothing she could do about it.

Dr Mowbray waged a constant war in the garden against couch grass, a hardy and abundant weed which he had inherited, along with the lupins, from old Miss Russell of Birkenshaw. It grew everywhere, it had creeping, tenacious roots, and it had proved, so far, impossible to get rid of. Dr Mowbray had told Fanny – who had already known, being at least as skilled a gardener as he was – that there was no point in pulling at the grass, which merely snapped off at the base of the stem; one must fetch a trowel, when one saw even a blade of the accursed stuff, and dig it out at the root.

That afternoon, Fanny had been weeding selectively. All the groundsel, sorrel, chickweed, pale willow-herb and small grasses had gone first, leaving the couch grass, which she called by its country name of quickens, for a trowel-assault at the end. It was while she was patiently digging a hole round a plant of the grass, making a little mound of soil at the side like a molehill, that she felt the trowel strike something hard. Clearing away the earth with her fingers, she pulled up a flat object which she thought at first glance must be a fossil, but immediately afterwards realised was not. Fanny had seen a collection of fossils at a Museum, and she knew that the stone which now lay on the palm of her hand, though it too bore a clearly traced design, owed its beauty to man, not to Nature. She knew this because the design, instead of being raised from the surface, as it is on a fossil, was cut deeply into the face. Fanny scraped away the dust and root-fibres which were clinging around it, and rubbed it on the knee of her jeans, then she held it up to the light and looked at it carefully. It was a flat, dark grey, rounded stone, about two inches across, polished beautifully by centuries of weathering. There was a hole near one end, through which you could thread a thong or a chain; the rest of the surface was covered with a design, engraved with incredible precision and attention to detail.

At first, Fanny supposed that the design was simply an abstract one, a lovely interweaving of lines such as one saw on ancient Christian stones in Scotland and in Ireland, where she had been once on holiday with her grandmother. But as she studied it, running her fingers lightly over the sharply incised lines, she realised that it was actually more like a maze, perfectly symmetrical and fitting itself to the shape of the stone. Starting at a point immediately below the hole, you could trace, with a pin or a pencil point, the path to the centre, which was represented by a round depression cut in a spiral. The stone was beautiful, but it was even more exciting to discover that it was also a game. Fanny had no idea how old it was, but her instinct told her it was very old indeed.

Always, in former days at Yesterlee, her first reaction to any find – the year's first kingcups in the water meadow, or a swallow's nest in the stable eaves – had been to fetch her grandmother to share it. Now she wanted to share the stone with her father, who was resting from his labours on their small, white summer seat, with a large mug of coffee balanced on his knee. But even as she started scrambling to her feet, for the second time in twenty-four hours something very peculiar happened to Fanny. For instead of running over to Dr Mowbray as she intended, sitting down on the seat beside him and saying, 'Look Dad! Isn't this marvellous?' she did something which she had no desire to do at all. She glanced furtively round to see if her father were watching her, and, when she was sure that he was not, slipped the stone into the pocket of her jersey. Then she walked straight indoors, and went upstairs to her bedroom. There she opened the cupboard where she hung her clothes, and, burrowing deeply, transferred the stone to the pocket of her winter coat which, in June, was hanging away at the back of the rail. She shut the cupboard carefully, went back downstairs to the garden, and started weeding again. But her heart was thumping painfully under her ribs, and a strange despair had seized her. For she knew that yet again she had behaved absurdly, against reason, and this time against her own inclination. But she could not persuade herself to go back upstairs, and fetch the stone to show to her father.

The next few days were nightmarish. Fanny got up in the morning, went to school, came home, did homework, helped in the house and went to bed, all with her mind in a frightened chaos. She could not eat, and she could not sleep. On Friday, Mrs Mowbray, who had observed with increasing anxiety her pale face and heavy eyes, sent her back to bed after breakfast, promising that she would telephone the school to explain.

'Though just how I am to explain, I don't know,' she remarked wearily to Hester, after Fanny had reluctantly gone upstairs again. 'Stuart says there's nothing medically the matter with her, and that time will sort things out, but it seems to me the poor kid is getting worse instead of better.'

'She hasn't been right all this week,' said Hester, who was spreading marmalade on her third slice of toast. 'Maybe it's the heat. I mean, you'd think she'd be getting over her old granny's death by now, wouldn't you?'

It seemed like eternity to Hester since old Mrs Mowbray had died, and Fanny had come to Hartslawhead.

'She'd get over it if she wanted to,' replied her mother, with a sigh.

Fanny, because she had been told to, spent the morning in bed. But she knew that staying in bed was the last thing likely to help her. She would have been better at school, with work to do, than lying alone in her bedroom, with horrible Bieldlaw blocking the window, and nothing to do but worry about the stone hidden in her overcoat pocket. Whenever she closed her eyes, she could see the round shape of the thing, blacker than the surrounding darkness, and when she opened them it was still there, no longer visible, but like a hard pain behind her forehead. It was bitter that the stone, which in the first moment of discovery had given her such an unaccustomed thrill of pleasure, should now have cast so thick a shadow over her mind, and make her feel that she no longer had complete control over her own actions and behaviour.

For she still wanted, more than anything else, to show her father the stone. In some strange way she felt that if only she did so, a spell would be broken, and the sharing would deliver her from danger. But no matter how often she told herself that all she had to do was wait till her father was alone in the sitting-room, fetch the stone from her coat pocket, and take it down to him, she could not do so. She had gone about all week with the thing boring a hole in her mind, while some inexplicable compulsion, at odds with her will, sapped her bodily strength and made her secretive as she had never been in her life before. It was terrifying.

At twelve o'clock, Fanny got out of bed, and went to the cupboard to fetch the stone. It was the first time she had touched it since the evening when she had found it in the garden. She took it over to her desk, and laid it carefully on the blotting pad, then she sat down and, with the point of a pencil, traced the curly, complicated path from the edge to the centre. She did this not once only, but many times, until she knew the pattern by heart. Then she turned the stone over, and from memory drew the maze again and again, all over the blotter. She had no idea why she did it, or why, when she heard Mrs Mowbray's key in the door, she snatched up the stone, and fled back across the floor to the cupboard, tossing skirts and frocks and jerseys aside in her panic anxiety to get the thing back into its dark hiding-place, before her stepmother came upstairs.

4. Morning Assembly

MEANWHILE, HESTER was having a wonderful time. Hers was a completely different nature from Fanny's, more cheerful and philosophical; when her long-divorced mother's remarriage forced her to leave her familiar, pleasant life in an English Midland town, and start a completely new life at Hartslawhead, she had taken the change easily in her stride. She liked her stepfather, and had quickly settled into her new home, making new friends at Millhall High School, and discreetly modifying her English accent. She had made overtures of friendship to the sad little Fanny, and when these were not returned, had gone back to minding her own business, and let the matter rest.

This was the third summer she had spent at Hartslawhead. She always enjoyed the summer term at school, with its tennis and athletics and sitting out of doors, and the long, clear evenings when she and Molly and the other girls would go to the park to watch the boys playing cricket. All her life she would associate the crack of ball against bat with the sound of young voices, clouds of midges dancing frantically under trees, and the sun going down red behind the shoulder of Bieldlaw. And this year it was even better, for there was the extra excitement of an end-of-term play in which she was taking part, and there were the English classes taken by Mr Lessing, who was the most fascinating person Hester had ever known.

It was not that he made any special fuss of her; she knew better than to expect that any teacher would do that. She had never been alone with him, and although he usually spent break in the dining-room with some of his pupils, he had never again come to a table where she and Molly were sitting. This made Hester a little cross and jealous, as she wanted to make a good impression on him, and was sure that no one else could discuss Drama with him as intelligently as she could. However, since he never came into the dining-room until after they had chosen their seats, she could not join his selected group without its being obvious that she was butting in. In class it was different. Armed with her mother's annotated copy of *The Merchant of Venice*, unopened since Mrs Mowbray's University days and now brought out of retirement, she was able to ask sharp questions and, as she put it, appear more clued-up than anyone else. One day Mr Lessing had praised her vowel sounds, remarking that of course she had the advantage of being English; this had pleased Hester, despite the enraged growls of everyone else in the class. However, it was generally agreed that Mr Lessing was a good teacher. He must be, as Hester remarked to her mother, since he was making even Molly enjoy Shakespeare.

There was also something about him which attracted Hester specially, without her being able to say exactly what it was. It might have had something to do with his eyes, bright and brown as they glanced around the class, or with his velvet voice, or the expressive movements of his long hands. Hester did not know, and it did not occur to her that perhaps she was a little in love with him. This was because she was more than a little in love with someone else; his name was Richard Simpson, School Captain and Captain of everything else as well. He lived opposite Hester in Birkenshaw Gardens, and since he sometimes cycled home with her, and usually took her as his partner at the Country Dancing Class, she assumed that he liked her too. Mr Lessing was different. Hester's principal reason, at the moment, for wanting to make a good impression on him was that she might then enlist his help in persuading her mother and Stuart to let her go to Drama School when she left Millhall High. They were at the moment determinedly against this idea, but Hester was an optimist, and she was sure that with Mr Lessing on her side, she would eventually make them change their minds. The problem was in arranging for them all to meet, and she had puzzled over it for some days before she heard, from Molly, that a Fifth Year girl called Janie Webster had already invited him to supper at her house, and that he had accepted.

'The cheek of it,' said Molly indignantly, and Hester did not disagree with her. Her own indignation, however, was muted by the realisation that here was the way out of her dilemma. If he had accepted Janie Webster's invitation, Mr Lessing could hardly refuse hers. And with the intention of issuing the invitation without delay, she went to school one morning. But when she got there, an incident occurred which put the idea out of her head for the rest of the day. The incident concerned Fanny.

Hester considered that Fanny, always queer, was getting queerer by the minute. She had heard of nervous breakdowns, and when she saw Fanny going about white-faced and absent-minded, jumping nervously at slight sounds and staring intently at nothing, she wondered vaguely if she might be having one. However, since Fanny had made it perfectly clear that she did not want to confide in Hester, and since there was, after all, a doctor in the house, she said nothing, and minded her own affairs as usual. There was one thing, however, about which she thought she ought to warn Fanny, and she did.

'Now, listen, Fan,' she said firmly one evening as they were going up to bed, 'you had better start showing your face at Morning Assembly. You haven't been there for weeks, and Mrs Weber has noticed, which serves you right for not wearing nice anonymous prison togs like the rest of us. She asked me this morning where you were, and I had to hum and haw, and say I thought you weren't feeling well, and had gone to the cloakroom. Whereas you were actually sitting in Stalag 3A doing your homework. Anyway, Ma Weber's got her beady eye on you, so I suggest you put in an appearance tomorrow.'

'Hell's teeth,' said Fanny irritably, kicking the wooden post at the top of the stair. 'I can't stand Morning Assembly – all these jazzy hymns, and silly prefects looking smug on the platform, and old Briggs bellyaching on about Netball scores, and not throwing sweetie papers in the fountain. Do I have to go, Hes?'

'Yes,' said Hester emphatically. 'It's a rule, and you're far too bolshie in general. You'll be getting me a bad name.'

Fanny scowled at her, then suddenly laughed, looking, Hester thought, fleetingly like another, unknown person.

'You're breaking my heart,' she said teasingly. 'Giving you a bad name! I think I'll go punk – that would really give you something to worry about. Oh, it's all right –' as Hester opened her mouth to protest '– I'll come tomorrow. Thanks for tipping me off.'

And the next day, she came. At five to nine, Hester, seated with Molly among the Fourth Year near the back of the School Hall, could see Fanny about a dozen rows in front of her, her red jersey and bright hair conspicuous among white blouses and heads which were varying shades of mouse.

'I told Fanny that Ma Weber was after her blood,' she remarked to Molly. 'She kicked up a bit of a fuss, but at least she's turned up today, thank goodness.'

Molly giggled.

'And she's making jolly sure Ma Weber sees she's here, too,' she pointed out. 'See where she's sitting – bang up against the staff chairs. They'll be able to spit at each other. You have to admit Fanny's colourful, Hes.'

'She's cracked,' said Hester seriously.

Molly was right. Fanny had come to Assembly to be seen by Mrs Weber, who was Deputy Head in charge of the girls, and in the hope that, once or twice seen, she might then be able to make herself scarce for another longish period. It was not that she was afraid of Mrs Weber, or cared much for her opinion, but she did not want reports of unco-operative behaviour on her part to reach her father's ears. If that happened, there would be a rumpus, and Fanny hated rumpuses, so it was wise to keep just the right side of the law. She had arrived in good time, and stationed herself on a chair at the end of a row, just across the narrow passage from the row of chairs, at right angles to the pupils' seats, where the teachers sat. Mrs Weber, begowned and self-important, always sat at the end of the row, so she must pass Fanny, who had taken off her grey blazer so that her jersey would be even more conspicuous. She occupied the time, while waiting for the proceedings to begin, by tracing with her toe on the polished floor the pattern of the maze stone. She was perpetually doing this, and drawing the pattern on scraps of paper, and on the covers of her exercise books; as often as not, she did not know she was doing it, and was surprised afterwards to notice that she had filled with the pattern spaces she thought were empty. Drawing with one's toe, or with one's finger on the desk, was less disturbing, because the line disappeared as quickly as it was made.

Presently the hubbub in the hall died away, as the staff and the prefects began to file in; Fanny rose to her feet with the rest as Mr Briggs, the Headmaster, took his place behind the reading-desk, and the Assembly was under way.

'Let us worship God, and sing . . . .'

Fanny looked up the hymn in her tattered School Hymnal, and fitted the words automatically to the bright, modern tune which was being banged out on the grand piano at the side of the platform.

>	'Thank you
>	for giving me the morning,
>	Thank you
>	for ev'ry day that's new . . . .'

Fanny stood up and sang. It was as well to let Mrs Weber see that she was not only there, but taking part. They had reached the last verse, however, before she allowed her eye to wander casually along the singing faces of the staff; she wanted to see Mrs Weber watching her, so that she could be sure her presence had been well and truly noted. Fanny knew most of the teachers by sight, although only a few actually taught her, like old Evans-the-Maths, Mrs Snow the Classics mistress, and the unlovable Miss Mole. It was therefore with a slight sense of being caught out that, before her glance reached Mrs Weber, she felt it meet the returning glance of a complete stranger, a thin young man in a leather jacket and a black polo-necked sweater. But there was nothing so very remarkable about it; Hester's Mr Lessing, her mind registered. But then, in that very instant, something very strange and frightening happened. It was ridiculous – but she could not stop looking at him. She did not want to look at him, but try as she might, she could not move her eyes from his face. And he looked back at her, with eyes unblinking, like a snake.

The hymn finished, and in the rustle and shuffle of sitting down they went on looking at each other. And then, as she tried in vain to turn her eyes to Mrs Weber, whose glum face would have been a welcome sight now, a terrible feeling of panic and nausea swept over Fanny. It was what she had felt as she cowered under the standing stone, that Friday evening a fortnight ago, when a young man came over the hill. Only now, in an enclosed space, it seemed a hundred times more intense, more suffocating. Only one thing she knew, as a blind slowly descended across the staring, mocking face, and she felt herself slip down unresisting from her chair – on both occasions her fear came from the same source. The young man in the denim suit, whose face she had not seen, and the new Drama teacher, whose face she would never forget, were the same person. Hester's favourite, Mr Nimmo Lessing.

When Fanny came round, she could see, fuzzily, a small square of white ceiling, with a wavering neon strip-light running down the middle of it. She focused her eyes on that, and slowly, although she still seemed to be far down in a kind of sleep, she became aware of herself and of her surroundings. She was lying on a sofa in Mrs Weber's office, and Mrs Weber and Hester were having a muted argument at her side.

'Look, she's beginning to come round. It's only a fainting fit, Hester – nothing to worry about. It happens all the time to girls around your age.' That was Mrs Weber.

'No. It's more than that. I'm sorry, but she hasn't been well for ages.' That was Hester. 'Her father's in school this morning, Mrs Weber – he gave us a lift in. He's here to give rubella injections to the First Year girls. I think he'd want to be told about this. I do – please.'

'Oh, very well.' It was obvious that Mrs Weber thought a great fuss was being made about nothing. 'Run along to the Ambulance Room and ask Dr Mowbray if he can spare a moment – although I dare say he'll think it quite unnecessary.'

But that was not what Dr Mowbray, when he came, appeared to think. He looked shrewdly at Fanny and felt her pulse, then he glanced at his watch and said hurriedly to Mrs Weber, 'I think I'll just run her home and see her into bed. She isn't going to be much use for lessons today. My first rubella lady isn't due till twenty to ten, and I'm sure I'll be forgiven if I'm a few minutes late.'

And Mrs Weber had to say, 'Yes, of course, Dr Mowbray. Whatever you say.'

Everything was still rather confused to Fanny, but she was aware of being taken out to the car park by her father, put into the car, and driven home through shiny wet streets lined with shoppers cowering under umbrellas. The weather had reverted to its mid-June normal. They did not talk; the only question Dr Mowbray asked was, 'Frances, when did you last have a good night's sleep?'

And Fanny, who was not at all pleased at the prospect of another day in bed, alone with her thoughts, replied repressively, 'I can't sleep. It must be the weather.'

The weather was blamed for everything, whether it was fair or foul.

She had to sit on a chair to take off her clothes and put on her nightdress, but once she had climbed into bed, and pulled the covers up to her chin, her head seemed to clear. When her father appeared, carrying two yellow pills and a glass of water, she was able to concentrate on what he was saying to her.

'People who don't get a night's sleep sometimes need a day's sleep,' he said, sitting down on the edge of the bed and giving her the pills and the water. 'Right, then. Big swallow.'

Fanny obeyed him. The pills slid down her throat, and he took the glass away. She knew that he had work to do, and that already the children would be queuing up outside the school Clinic, but she did rather hope he would go on sitting there for a little. And he did, looking at her with eyes that were blue like her grandmother's, and like her own. There was silence for a few moments, then he said, 'Frances, is there anything you want to tell me?'

He sometimes called her Frances, though no one else ever did. He had not wanted her to be called Fanny at all, but she had given the name to herself as a little girl and it had stuck, as such names do. Hester occasionally wondered how anyone could bear to be called Fanny Mowbray, but Fanny herself never gave it a thought. She looked up at her father now, and longing welled up in her to tell him everything, about the maze-stone, and the young man, and how afraid she was. But still the urge to secrecy was upon her, and she said, 'No,' hopelessly.

'Because if there is anything – other than still feeling low about Granny's death – you ought to tell me, you know. It's what I'm here for.'

He paused, and waited, and for a long moment Fanny struggled with her need to get started. If only she could get started, she would surely be able to go on, and share her burden with him, and get relief. And she very nearly did; she was actually opening her mouth to say, 'Well, you see, one night I was up on Bieldlaw,' when suddenly the sheer incredibility of the whole thing overcame her, and the words died on her lips. For how could any sensible adult – and her father was the most sensible of men – come to the conclusion that what she felt was anything but a sign that she was going crazy? Granny alone would have been an exception, Granny who knew, and had taught Fanny to know, that the world is full of strangeness which sensible people are prevented by their sense from perceiving, let alone understanding. Her father, trained to take the scientific view, and so long away from his country upbringing, would be bound to conclude that his daughter was mentally disturbed, and would react as a doctor – the last thing Fanny wanted to happen, for she knew that madness was not her problem.

So she shook her head, repeating, 'No,' and adding, 'I'm all right, Dad. I like it here. I just miss Granny.'

Dr Mowbray sighed, and touched her cheek with his forefinger.

'I know,' he said. 'It's very difficult, and at the time it's no help to be told you'll feel better later on. I remember thinking that when your mother died. On the other hand, it's true. Life has to go on, and we can't be for ever grieving. I'm sure the dead wouldn't want us to. What you have to remember, Frances, is that Granny was close on eighty. She'd had a long, active life, and she died the way we'd all like to die, quickly and without pain. She certainly wouldn't want you to spend your days sorrowing. I don't mean you should try to forget – you never will. But if you don't fight all the time to stay miserable, the way you remember will change. You'll come to remember Granny and the old life with love and happiness. Wouldn't that be better?'

'Yes,' Fanny said.

She had heard it all before. It made no difference. For how could you ever explain to anyone that you were not only sick and lonely for a person, but haunted by the memory of an ancient house, with swallows nesting now, this very summer, in its eaves, and roses that went on blooming in that garden, not caring that you weren't there to see them, would never be there to see them again, as long as you lived? For the house was sold. Mowbrays had no place there any more.

'I think I'll go to sleep now,' Fanny said.

Dr Mowbray stood up, and drew the covers around her.

'Yes, go to sleep,' he said. 'I'll be back as soon as I can. And try to remember that you still live with people who care about you, and want you to be happy.'

Fanny's fear of another day of lonely anxiety was not realised, as the yellow pills had effect almost immediately. Dr Mowbray had scarcely closed the bedroom door and gone downstairs, when a merciful shawl of darkness floated down and covered her.

5. *The Invitation*

ASSISTED BY two more pills, Fanny slept the night through as well, and awoke next morning to find Hester in her room, clearing away the books on her bedside table to make room for a breakfast tray. Fanny pushed away the bedclothes and sat up, wondering for a moment what on earth was going on. Then she remembered. She had fainted at Assembly. But was it yesterday, or one day ages ago? She could not tell. She watched Hester, dressed in her new Indian print skirt and black T-shirt, which were supposed to look theatrical, pulling back the curtains to admit a pure grey stream of morning light.

'Is it Saturday?' Fanny asked uncertainly.

'All day,' Hester agreed. She turned round, and observed Fanny with keen eyes and a comically pursed mouth. 'How do you feel now?' she enquired. 'I'm sure all that sleep can't be good for anyone.'

'Better, I think,' Fanny replied.

Her glance fell on the breakfast tray, and she knew at once that Hester had prepared it. Alison, always short of time for the hundred and one jobs she had to do, would have brought her a mug of coffee and a piece of toast and marmalade on the battered tin tray with an advertisement for Colman's mustard on it. Hester had fetched a nice wicker tray from the cupboard in the dining-room, and spread a tray cloth on it. Fanny had a cup and saucer, and a pot of coffee, toast in a rack, and butter and marmalade in tiny dishes. Hester had also provided the local newspaper, neatly folded, and a little vase of flowers. Fanny was pleased, and embarrassed at the same time. She looked at Hester shyly and said, 'You shouldn't have.'

'Yes, I should,' contradicted Hester. She paused, then added, 'I'm sorry about your faint. I feel it was partly my fault, because I was the one who pestered you about going to Morning Assembly.'

'Don't be daft,' said Fanny witheringly.

'Well, O.K. But I did. Actually, when I saw you hitting the floor, I thought you'd done it on purpose to annoy Ma Weber. But not when I saw the revolting colour of your face.'

'Don't tell me,' said Fanny. 'I can imagine. Do you know, I never thought of doing it on purpose. I don't think I could fake a faint, unfortunately. Could you?'

'I might – on the stage, you know,' Hester replied. 'But I couldn't go green on purpose, that's asking too much. What made you faint, Fan?'

'I don't know,' said Fanny, hoping she did not sound as uncomfortable as she felt. It would be so terrible if Hester suspected . . . .

'May I have the tray on my knee?' she asked hastily, to change the subject.

'Sure,' said Hester, who suspected nothing, and gave it to her. 'Now eat it all – it will help to build you up.'

'Into a skeleton,' said Fanny dolefully. But she spread some butter and marmalade on a slice of toast, and thought the coffee smelt delicious.

Hester laughed. Sometimes, she thought, Fanny could be quite witty.

'Well, if you'll excuse me, I must be off,' she said. 'Mother says you're to stay in bed till she comes back. She's gone to the hairdresser to have her haystack done – her words, not mine. I'm going up to the school – we're rehearsing *The Shoemaker's Holiday* this morning at ten o'clock, and Mr Lessing is coming to see it, so I hope it goes well.'

To cover her fright at the sound of that name, Fanny said lightly, 'Has Molly managed to get her lines into her head yet?'

Hester rolled her eyes ceiling-wards.

'Kid,' she said emphatically, 'Molly will never get her lines into her head. Never. And she's only got three. Well – I'll leave you to divert yourself with the "Squeak". It makes fascinating reading. The Council has given permission to the man from Wigan to go ahead with the quarry, and Stuart's off to the surgery with a face like the wrath of God. I'm glad he's not sticking a needle in me this morning. See you, Fanny.'

And she went, singing all the way downstairs.

Left alone, Fanny drank some coffee, finished her piece of toast, noticed with surprise that she was still hungry, and ate another piece. Then she put the tray aside, folded the newspaper with the article about the quarry uppermost, and settled herself to read.

It appeared that the District Council had decided to grant permission to a Mr Joseph Pickering of Wigan Stoneholdings Ltd., in Lancashire, to quarry whinstone from the south side of Bieldlaw – that was the Birkenshaw Gardens side. To begin with, the workings would employ twenty-five men, rising to a hundred and fifty when production reached its height. The Convener of the District Council, the article said, was delighted by the prospect of a hundred and fifty jobs for local lads at a time of high unemployment, while Mr Pickering, smiling benignly from a photograph, gave an assurance that the disturbance and loss of amenity would be so slight as to be 'not worth talking about'. The last paragraph of the report stated briefly that a representative of the Millhall and Hartslawhead Civic Amenities Council had expressed disquiet at the plan, and that the matter of objections would be raised at the next meeting of the District Council on 20th June.

Fanny read the article twice, then tossed the paper on to

the floor. Really, she hardly knew what she thought. She had forgotten about the quarry, and her parents' anxiety, because she had had, to put it mildly, other things on her mind, and even now, when it seemed the quarry would become a reality, she did not care very much. Although she would not have chosen to have a noisy, dusty excavation on Bieldlaw, she did not belong to Hartslawhead, and she could not feel the shock and anger of a person who had played on that hillside as a child, or perhaps walked there with a lover on summer evenings long ago. Nor did she feel the outrage of incomers like Dr and Mrs Mowbray, who had bought expensive houses only yards from where the quarry was to be sited. A few weeks ago, she would certainly have regretted the loss of her quiet green place, but now her feelings about Bieldlaw had changed. Since the night when Nimmo Lessing had come down through the trees, the place had scared her, and she was sure that she would never want to go up to the standing stones again. Therefore, they could make a quarry or not, as they liked; it made no odds to her. Indeed, she thought, if the quarry should prove such a nuisance that her parents decided to sell their house and move elsewhere, that would suit her perfectly. Sometimes she felt that her only salvation lay in running away from whatever enchantment had taken hold of her. But at the same time, a clearer, more robust part of her mind told her that the solution was not going to be as easy as that.

Although Fanny's collapse had driven the matter temporarily from her mind, Hester had not forgotten her intention to invite Mr Lessing to supper. During the next few days, however, the opportunity never seemed to present itself. She had hoped to be able to speak to him alone after the Saturday morning rehearsal in which, she reckoned, she had performed rather splendidly, but Molly clung to her like a limpet, and by the time she had disengaged herself, Mr Lessing was disappearing out of the school yard on his bicycle. After Monday's lesson, he had shot off to a staff meeting, and after Wednesday's some of the boys had crowded round, hoping to persuade him to take part in the

Staff *v*. Pupils Cricket Match. Hester had another class, and couldn't wait.

Meanwhile, however, she was finding Mr Lessing more and more agreeable; he was becoming almost as attractive to her as he was repellent to Fanny. Perhaps the fact that Richard Simpson had left school early, and gone off to Holland for the summer, had something to do with it, but not much. What she felt for Mr Lessing was something quite different, less intimate in one way, because he was older, and a teacher, but also more satisfying. She began to crave his attention, and would feel absurdly delighted when, in class, he sometimes seemed to single her out to share with him some interesting point in the play which he inferred was beyond the grasp of the others. But he still did not pay her any special attention outside the class-room, and she could scarcely believe her luck, on Thursday afternoon after school, when, as she was saying goodbye to Molly at Molly's gate in Bieldlaw Court, Mr Lessing came rattling along on his ancient bicycle. He mounted the pavement when he saw the two girls, and came to a halt with his front wheel wedged in the hedge. He was wearing a dark blue shirt, open at the neck, and his silver medallion was swinging to and fro like a pendulum.

'Hello, ladies,' he said. 'I didn't know you lived in these parts.'

'Do you?' enquired Molly. 'I haven't seen you around here before either.'

'I'm in lodgings in Lanark Road,' he told her. 'Landlady by the name of Mrs MacPhee. Very genteel. "Would you like a nice boilt egg to your tea, Mr Lessing? I'd of got you a steak, or a nice bit of haddock, only the butcher and the fishmonger was shut. It's the half day, you ken".' He imitated the high, sing-song West of Scotland voice perfectly, and Molly, who spoke exactly the same way herself, was overwhelmed with amusement.

'And where do you live, Hester?' he went on, turning to her with a friendly smile.

'At eleven, Birkenshaw Gardens,' Hester told him.

'Come on, then. I'll walk with you,' he said. 'Goodbye, Miss Molly. See you at school.'

Hester tried not to see Molly's disappointed face as she walked away. It would have spoiled her own delight in this, the moment she had been waiting for.

Long after, Hester would remember the ten minutes' walk between Molly's house and hers as the time when she fell completely in love with Nimmo Lessing. For the first time, he made himself irresistible, telling her how much he had admired her acting at the rehearsal for the school play, asking her about her plans for the future, promising not only to speak to her parents, but also to people he knew in London, who taught at a famous Drama School. Hester could scarcely believe her ears; indeed, her head was in such a whirl that it was all she could do, when the time came to part from him outside her gate, to deliver her invitation coherently.

'Mr Lessing, I was wondering – could you possibly come to supper at our house on Sunday evening? I'd like my mother and father to meet you – well, he's my stepfather, actually, but he's awfully nice. Please do come.'

'Yes. Thanks, I'd like that very much,' Mr Lessing responded immediately, 'if you're sure your mother won't mind. Hadn't you better ask her first?'

'No. I know it will be all right. Mother likes having people in at the week-ends, when she has time to do the cooking. She's a very good cook.'

'That'll be a nice change. At Mrs MacPhee's it's a boiled egg for every occasion, except when it's a boiled egg.'

Hester laughed.

'I'll tell mother no boiled eggs,' she promised. 'Can you come about seven?'

'About seven,' he agreed, and hopping on his bicycle, rattled away.

When Fanny heard that Mr Lessing had been invited to supper, her immediate feelings were of horror and despair, and although all week she had been annoyed by remarks about her paleness, she was glad now that no one seemed to notice her paling even further. But when she had gone out into the garden, leaving the rest of the family watching tennis on television, she realised quickly enough that if she did not pull herself together, and make an overwhelming effort to behave normally, she would draw to herself attention of a very unwelcome kind. And this man, Nimmo Lessing, would have won, without even having had to fight. It had only just occurred to her to wonder what he was trying to do, and what he hoped to gain by reducing her to a state of terror; he might of course be straightforwardly evil, but Fanny had an intuition that there was more to it than that. But anyway, she told herself, as she sat curled up in a corner of the summer seat, he was not going to have his way. A sudden, gritty determination had entered her, and she was not going to be bullied any more. Somehow, she was going to fight back; Granny would have expected her to be brave.

Fanny thought a lot about her grandmother during the next day or two, with less pain about her heart than usual. For the first time since she came to Hartslawhead, she seemed simply to be drawing strength from the memory of that calm, understanding old woman, who had lived close to nature, and had known so much of the mystery underlying what we call normal life.

Sunday morning came, and while Alison prepared a casserole for supper, and Hester made a chocolate mousse for Mr Lessing, Fanny went out to water the plants in the greenhouse. She had the feeling of a person about to go into hospital for an operation, a feeling of fright kept by great mental effort under a surface of calm. But at least she was managing to keep the surface calm, and she now thought that perhaps she could continue to do so in the presence of Nimmo Lessing. If only she had some small protection . . . . While she was watering the tomatoes, her father came out and asked whether she felt up to doing a little weeding.

'Of course,' Fanny assured him. 'I feel fine now, Dad.'

'Down by the fence, then, dearie. There are lupins, and that betony stuff, and heaven knows what else, all rearing their ugly heads in my asparagus bed. I'd give you a hand, only I have to go over to Rory's, to help get the Great Protest under way. We're organising a door-to-door petition – you'll have to sign, Fan.'

'Delighted, if you think it'll make any difference,' said

Fanny sceptically. 'What else are you going to do?'

'Oh, we're preparing reports on aspects of health and amenity, and organising a public meeting, and writing to our M.P. and the Secretary of State for Scotland.' He grinned at Fanny, and added in a whisper, 'Don't breathe a word to Alison, but I'm thoroughly enjoying myself. It must be in my blood. I love a fight.'

'Do you think you'll win?' Fanny asked curiously.

'I haven't a clue,' said Dr Mowbray cheerfully, and disappeared whistling round the corner of the house.

'I love a fight,' repeated Fanny to herself, as she finished watering, and put the can back on the shelf. 'A fat lot he knows about it, that's all.'

She fetched the dustbin lid and went down the garden, forcing herself to look up straight at Bieldlaw for the first time in three weeks.

The hill rose dramatically before her, a dark, brooding green, except on its eastern edge, where the rays of a wet sun made a lighter streak, which struck upwards towards the trees. There were some children, in a moving straggle of colour, climbing towards the standing stones, and it all looked perfectly normal, Fanny had to admit. But underneath, the creepy feeling persisted. She squatted down, and began to pull up the seedling lupins, little green hands opening among the darker feathers of asparagus.

Fanny had been brought up by a gardener who was also a naturalist. She knew a weed as a weed, but she also knew it as a flower, which could have been left alone if it had only had the sense to grow in a hedgerow, not in a vegetable garden. At first, it had surprised her that so many of the woodland species which grew in the country places around Yesterlee, also appeared in her father's suburban garden at Hartslawhead. But Dr Mowbray had pointed out that, sixty years ago, the country around Hartslawhead had been almost as open and unspoiled as that around Yesterlee. Only Yesterlee was more fortunate, because it had no great city squatting across the valley, stretching out dirty tentacles, blighting field and wood. But the flowers went on growing, somewhere, anywhere.

So, as Fanny pulled up the weeds, she named them:

betony, herb bennet, St John's wort. Strange but nice, she reflected, to think that all of these had grown by the roadside, just outside the gates of Yesterlee. And they had something in common, if only she could remember what it was. She racked her brains for a while, then it came to her. Long ago in the country places, people believed that if you had these three plants growing near the entrance to your house, they would turn away evil spirits.

If anyone had asked Fanny, three weeks ago, whether she believed in evil spirits, she would probably have said that she had no way of knowing whether they existed or not. But she would not have laughed contemptuously at the idea, as more sophisticated young people, like Hester, would have done. Fanny had lived all her life, till now, with a woman who, three hundred years ago, would have been called a witch. If she had never thought of her grandmother in that way, it was partly because she associated witches with broomsticks and steeple hats, and partly because her grandmother represented the power of healing, not the power of destruction. But now, when evil threatened, Fanny recognised it for what it was, and because she knew that herbs could provide help for many bodily illnesses, she did not rule out the idea that they could help against danger unseen.

So she selected from the pile of weeds some pink sprigs of betony and a spike of St John's wort, and bound them to the yellow-starred herb bennet with a blade of strong grass. Then she pushed the flowers into her pocket and went on weeding, feeling stronger than she had done for a long time.

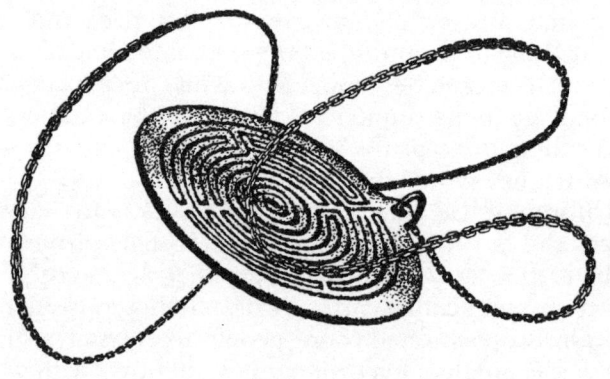

6. Supper on Sunday

EVENING CAME. Hester laid the table in the dining-room with the same loving care she had lavished on Fanny's breakfast tray. She was the kind of person who can always express feeling best in practical ways. She was wearing her Indian skirt, with a red blouse which Dr Mowbray had given her as a reward for passing a Maths. exam for the first time in her life, and looked, Fanny thought, like a real actress. Fanny had taken off her red jersey, because it had earth on its cuffs, and had put on a pink one which she kept for emergencies. She had taken her wild flowers out of her pocket, and put them into a little velvet draw-string bag which usually held her mother's gold locket and chain; on an impulse that she did not understand, she had also threaded the mysterious maze stone on to the silk string, before putting it round her neck. She could feel it, cold and heavy against her skin, under the loose woollen folds of her jersey; it was not an object which had given her any pleasure, and it was odd that she should feel protected by it now. But she did, as she sat on the sofa, watching the pendulum on Dr Mowbray's treasured wall clock wipe out the minutes before seven. She wished the man would come, and have done.

The clock chimed, and three minutes later Mr Nimmo Lessing came cruising down the street on his bicycle, propped it carelessly against the hedge, and rang the doorbell. Fanny heard his voice in the hall, and a minute after that he was in the room. For a terrible instant, she thought she felt the old panic begin to suffocate her, but then, by a deliberate act of will, she controlled it, and looked him straight in the eye. He looked back, and as she saw his reptilian stare waver uncertainly, she knew she was protected. But whether by the flowers, or the stone, or her own determination to fight, there was no way of knowing.

What always astonished Fanny, when she was able to look back on these events from another time and place, was that no one that night, apart from Nimmo Lessing and herself, seemed to notice the strife between them. For her, and, she knew, for him, it filled the air as with beating wings. She made herself shake hands with him, and controlled the urge to withdraw her hand sharply from contact with his skin. She watched from the sofa as he accepted whisky from Dr Mowbray, and answered Mrs Mowbray's polite questions about his lodgings, and how he was enjoying his work at Millhall High. He was wearing a tweed tie with his black shirt and leather jacket, and, if the truth were told, looked considerably less stagey than Hester did. Hester sat on the arm of the sofa, looking pleased, indeed, to Fanny's suddenly sharp eyes, a little more than pleased. There had been teachers to supper before, and Hester had never looked so bright about the eyes, nor so rosy-cheeked. Mr Lessing drew her into the conversation with lightly complimentary remarks about the school play; on the surface he was behaving impeccably, Fanny observed. He did not look at her, or speak to her, yet she knew that underneath his silky politeness, he was just as aware of her as she was of him. It was as if waves of hostility were washing to and fro between them, only this time he could not quench her with his mocking stare. This unnerved him, and Fanny rejoiced to see him unnerved. But before she was tempted to give herself away by any small sign of triumph, Mrs

Mowbray called them into the dining-room, and they took their places at the table.

Fanny never talked much at meal times, so her silence now passed unremarked. Seated between her father and Alison, she watched Hester and Nimmo Lessing through a grove of tall candles which Hester had lit in the centre of the table, though it was still broad daylight. To anyone but Fanny, the guest would have appeared perfectly at ease, as he ate pork casserole and cauliflower, and told Mrs Mowbray how wonderful it was to eat a well cooked meal for once. Only Fanny was sure he was not at ease. His brown eyes, which could look so intelligent and polite when he looked at Dr Mowbray, so gentle and friendly when he turned to Alison and Hester, went brightly hard in the instant when, almost furtively, he looked at her, then quickly looked away again. Fanny felt pleased, but she did not allow herself to relax. She watched Nimmo Lessing as one might a quiescent but unconfined snake.

The conversation began boringly. All through the casserole-and-cauliflower course, the talk was all about teaching, and amateur dramatic clubs, and how *The Shoemaker's Holiday* was an original and pleasing choice for the end-of-term play, but *Ralph Roister Doister* might have been better. Then, after the meat plates had been cleared away, the coffee cups prepared, and Hester's chocolate mousse placed on the table, Dr Mowbray suddenly turned towards the visitor and said, 'Hester tells me you had family in these parts at one time. Any of them still around?'

It would have needed concentration such as Fanny was giving him to detect the flash of uncertainty which crossed Nimmo Lessing's eyes. If he had given this information before – and he had, walking home with Hester and Molly from Friday night's rehearsal – he certainly didn't want to expand upon it now. Yet he replied unconcernedly enough, 'No. That's to say, I did once have family around here, but I don't think there are any still around. Certainly none known to me.'

'Ah. I just wondered,' Dr Mowbray replied. He was not being curious, only trying to make conversation. 'There are Lessings in Millhall – two brothers, Reuben and David.

They have a sawmill – old established business, but not doing too well these days, like everything else. I thought there might be some connection there.'

'No,' said Nimmo Lessing quickly. 'No, it was my mother's side of the family. Gordon was the name. I suppose there are a lot of them around too?'

'I couldn't say,' said Dr Mowbray, and the subject was dropped.

Fanny ate her chocolate mousse, and watched Nimmo Lessing regain the little poise he had lost. The conversation survived several attempts by Hester to divert it back into theatrical channels; Fanny felt sorry for her, as she had had relayed to her, in the privacy of the greenhouse, all the nice things Mr Lessing had said about Hester's acting, and how he was going to take her part with Stuart and Alison. If so, he seemed in no hurry to do so. Instead, as if he were now anxious to control the subjects discussed, he was professing great interest in Dr Mowbray's attempts to grow asparagus, and went on to question Mrs Mowbray closely about her rather humdrum job teaching Latin and Scripture at a Boys' Prep. School in Millhall. Fanny felt that her father did not particularly like their guest, but that might have been wishful thinking. The Mowbrays were a conscientiously polite couple.

It was not until they were back in the sitting-room, having coffee, that, as usually happens eventually among strangers, all the obvious topics of conversation had been used up. It was then that Dr Mowbray casually picked up Friday's copy of the *Millhall and District Courier* from the end of the coffee table, and, pointing to a banner headline, RESIDENTS FIGHT BACK, said to Nimmo Lessing, 'You wouldn't like to join a Citizens' Action Committee, by any chance, would you? There are plans afoot to blow the top off our private mountain.'

It was said purely to keep talk going, and mild incredulity, or disapproval, might have been expected as reactions from a stranger, followed by a light-hearted refusal to get involved. Nimmo Lessing's reaction was quite different, and this time it was not only Fanny who noticed. A fork-like frown appeared between his eyebrows, his shoulders stiffened, and he stretched out a fidgety, demanding hand for the newspaper.

'Your private mountain?' he rapped out. 'What on earth do you mean?'

Mrs Mowbray was looking at him in surprise, Hester in apprehension, but Dr Mowbray tossed the paper over to him and said calmly, 'Bieldlaw. The hill behind us, you know. They want to quarry whinstone – a hundred thousand tons in the first five years. There'll hardly be a hill left when they've finished. What do you think of that, then?'

Whatever Nimmo Lessing thought, he was evidently very upset indeed. He had gone as white as a sheet, and as he read, he kept muttering things like, 'Why did nobody tell me about this?' and, 'Monstrous, impossible,' and, 'It must be stopped.' His dismay seemed excessive, considering that he had only been a few weeks in the town. But then he looked up, and saw them all staring at him. He made a great effort, and pulled himself together. But what he said sounded feeble, and it was not only Fanny who thought so.

'Sorry,' he said. 'It just came as a bit of a shock. I've so often heard my grandmother describe how she used to play on Bieldlaw when she was a little girl. And it's such a pleasant spot – an oasis, don't you think, in all this concrete and tar macadam?'

'Your grandmother,' repeated Dr Mowbray. 'Mrs Gordon?'

'Um, yes. Of course, her family left here and went south years ago – you wouldn't have heard of them, I'm sure.'

'Have some more coffee, Mr Lessing,' said Mrs Mowbray into the silence that followed. 'And Fanny darling, it's time you were off to bed.'

Fanny was thankful now to mutter goodnight, and get herself out of the room, for her head was reeling, and she doubted that she could much longer appear calm in front of the others. For something very odd had just happened, something which made her more aware than ever that she was caught up in something very dangerous and queer. For as Nimmo Lessing had bent forward quickly to seize the newspaper, his silver pendant, which he had been wearing concealed under his tie, swung forward, and dangled for a moment right in front of Fanny's eyes. And before he had put out his hand to cover it again, she had recognised the design beaten out on it, one she knew better than any design she had ever seen in her life. The pendant was a replica in silver of the maze stone.

7. At the Ring of Trees

EXHAUSTED YET in a whirl of excitement, Fanny washed and cleaned her teeth, put on her nightdress and climbed into bed. Downstairs in the hall, Nimmo Lessing's voice was audible, thanking Mrs Mowbray for a lovely evening; Fanny heard the rattle of his bicycle's mudguards as he rode off down the street, then the welcome click of the lock on the front door, shutting him out. Hester and her mother came up to bed; Fanny lay in the darkness listening to their familiar night-time conversation.

'Hester! Hurry up in the bathroom. What on earth are you doing?'

Sometimes the reply was, 'Taking my eye make-up off,' or, 'Putting in my rollers.' Tonight it was, 'Rubbing Dermitex on these damn spots. Lord, I look a mess.'

'Well, get a move on. You'll look a worse mess in the morning, if you haven't had enough sleep. And so will I.'

'Sorry, sorry. I'm just coming.'

It was all so normal that it was difficult to accept that something very abnormal was threatening to invade their ordinary family life, but it was; for the first time, and with a feeling of chill, Fanny realised that Hester was at risk too – more at risk, in fact, because she thought Nimmo Lessing was wonderful, and she was completely off guard. Presently silence fell over the house, and in it Fanny lay awake for a while, wondering what she must do.

To begin with, she could only think of what she could not do, which was to confide in anyone. Who would believe that her story was anything but a tissue of nonsense? Her father? Alison? Hester? Their faces passed before the eye of her mind, concerned, sympathetic, incredulous. The Police? That idea was too silly to waste time on. And in any case – what did the story amount to, when she put it into words? That the appearance of one young man – a teacher, for Heaven's sake – had twice made her feel faint and frightened, and that the design on his silver pendant happened to be the same as one on a stone she had turned up in the garden. And that she had tried to protect herself from the evil eye by carrying magic flowers, like some superstitious country girl. That was what it all amounted to, when you summed it up. Fanny knew in her heart that in this affair feelings were far more important than what appeared to be facts, but she also knew that no one else would agree with her. So she was in this on her own. That was point one. Point two was that, for the moment, there was nothing she could do, except be watchful and wait; watch Nimmo Lessing, and wait for him to make the next move.

Not long after she had come to this conclusion, she heard the clock downstairs chiming twelve. Then she fell asleep.

During the next few days, life went on much as usual. Fanny did not see Mr Lessing at Assembly on the two mornings when she thought it would be prudent to put in an appearance; after Sunday evening, she knew she would be all right, even if he were there. She did not even have time to think about him very much, as she was having to sit class exams for which she had made very little preparation, so that her evenings were spent frantically trying to cram into a few hours work which should have been spread over all the weeks since March. Part of her did not care whether she did well or not, but another, stronger part was too proud to relish the idea of being at the bottom of the class.

Hester's exams were over last month, and for her, classes and rehearsals were going on normally. She was disappointed that Mr Lessing had not taken the opportunity to speak warmly to her parents about her future in the theatre; she was aware that the evening had not been a complete success. However, she hoped that there would be another, more fruitful, meeting later, and meanwhile, she was happy enough. Mr Lessing had taken to walking or cycling home with her and Molly after school, and this was to Hester's liking, as she always had him to herself for a precious ten minutes between Molly's house and hers. Then he would give her fascinating glimpses of his past life – he had, he said, worked in the circus as well as in the theatre. He had ridden in a rodeo in Montana, and been a stunt rider for a film company. He had been a tap dancer, and a gypsy fortune-teller on the pier at Blackpool. Hester, who had led a very sheltered life, was fascinated. She was now completely in love with him, and although she knew how angrily her parents would have disapproved, she longed for just one little sign that he cared for her, too. But Nimmo Lessing was too prudent for that, and Hester had to be content with the walks home, and banter shared with Molly, who was quite unaware of being a gooseberry, and thought he was 'a scream'.

Fanny's exams lasted through four days of perfect summer weather, and on the evening of the last day, Dr Mowbray arrived home at six o'clock saying, 'Now, then – who's going to climb Bieldlaw with me after supper? We've been talking about it for long enough, and it's going to be a lovely clear evening. The view from the top will be magnificent.'

He stood at the entrance to the kitchen, leaning his long back against the doorpost, looking at them expectantly.

Mrs Mowbray, who was peeling potatoes, stirring sauce and reading a letter, all more or less at the same time, gave him a harrassed look, and said, 'Not tonight, darling.

Sorry. I've got a pile of ironing to do, and my feet are tired.'

Hester tried to look regretful, but couldn't quite manage it.

'Sorry. Rehearsal,' she said.

But Fanny, somewhat to her own surprise, said, 'I'll come with you, Dad. I'd like to.'

And it was true. A fortnight ago, nothing would have dragged her on to that hillside. Indeed, she had made up her mind that she would never set foot on it again. But since she had managed to control her terror of Nimmo Lessing, her fear and dislike of the hill had become controllable too. And she felt safe with her father. He had that effect on a person, and sometimes still Fanny was tempted to tell him the whole story, just for the relief of being contradicted by him, and laughed at, and told not to be a silly pussy. She resisted because she knew the relief would not last; she was not a silly pussy, and what she was involved in was no laughing matter.

So, after supper, while Hester went off to her rehearsal at the school, and Alison settled to her ironing in front of the television, Fanny and her father left the house by the back door, climbed over the fence, and began the ascent of Bieldlaw. It was a still evening, windless and clear, with the sun dipping towards the west in a thinly blue sky. There was a paring of moon overhead, but it would not be dark for a long time. They went up slowly but steadily over the sheep-cropped grass, stopping occasionally to get their breath; when they got to the standing stones they sat down for a few minutes, and shared a bar of chocolate which Dr Mowbray took out of his pocket.

'Good for energy, bad for teeth,' he said.

Fanny broke her half into four pieces and ate them slowly, looking down on Birkenshaw Gardens which, even from this height, looked like a long string of identical dolls' houses, set in tablecloth-sized gardens. A few families, like themselves, were growing vegetables and flowers; lupins, carnations, pansies and lavender spilled colour over the little plots. Most, however, had settled for lawn, with perhaps a tiny rock garden, because it was easier, and left more time for the golf course.

Suddenly Fanny said, 'Look, Dad! I've never noticed that before.'

'What, love?'

'Well, look at the grass, in the Allens' garden, and the Lowes'. You can see where the walls of that old house must have been – in fact, it looks as if the foundations are still there, under the grass.'

Dr Mowbray's eye followed Fanny's pointing finger, and he too saw the huge and wide rectangular ridge, crossed at right angles by other ridges not so wide, showing where the remains of the old house's foundations still lay, under the surface of the grass.

'Good for you, Fan,' said her father. 'Of course, you're quite right.' He paused, then added, 'Think of walls rising there, to the height they must have done. The back of the place must have been only feet away from the hillside. Damned unhealthy, if you ask me.'

'Yes,' agreed Fanny, 'and silly, when they had plenty of room. Did you once tell me you could remember it, Dad?'

'In the vaguest way, I can. I don't know that I ever saw more of it than crumbling chimneys, and a bit of sagging roof. The hedge at the front had grown to an incredible height.'

'They shouldn't have pulled it down,' said Fanny, who was against the pulling down of old houses on principle.

'I don't think they could have done anything else, it was in such a state,' Dr Mowbray told her. 'Nobody would ever have lived in it again. It had a bad reputation.'

'What sort of bad reputation?'

'Oh, ghosties and ghoulies,' replied her father carelessly. 'And there was some story about a young man being murdered and buried under the floor. Nonsense, probably. Let's push on, shall we?'

They climbed again, not talking, to save their breath; Fanny thought of the old house, and wondered what it had looked like, and was sad that it had been allowed to fall into ruin, and end its days unwanted and unloved. She could not imagine such a fate overtaking the old house at Yesterlee, but then nothing terrible had ever happened there. She felt sure that its benevolent spell would fall upon its owners in the future, as it had upon those of the past. Fanny did not notice that for the first time since she left it, she was thinking of Yesterlee naturally, without bitterness and great pain; she was happy to think that others would love it, and protect it, as in a different way it would protect them. Quite suddenly, they came to the ring of trees.

For all her previous feeling that Bieldlaw was an odd place, Fanny was completely unprepared for the strangeness of its summit. There was no obvious reason why the atmosphere inside the circle of wind-crippled oaks should be so very different from that outside, but it was so; Fanny knew that her father felt it too, because when she slipped her hand into his, he did not seem surprised, but held on to it firmly with his strong fingers. It was suddenly icy cold, and there was a stillness which had nothing to do with peace. Hand in hand they wandered among the trees, looking at the view which included nine counties, stretching from the Perthshire mountains to the golden sunset sea beyond the Clyde. It was astonishingly beautiful, but somehow the thrall of the hilltop made it hard to concentrate on anything beyond.

Presently, still holding Dr Mowbray's hand, Fanny turned inward to the bald green cone which formed the centre of the ring. At least, it was bald on the Birkenshaw side, which faced west, where the sun was now going down in a tangle of rose and orange ribbons. But when they moved round to the eastern side, which looked out towards the Pentlands and the misty farmlands of Lothian, Fanny saw that the grass was strangely riven by a stone scar, about two yards long and six inches wide, running vertically to the line of the trees. Nothing grew for about a foot on either side of it, and the redness of the exposed earth made it look like a wound.

'What a peculiar thing,' said Fanny in a low voice. 'What do you suppose it is?'

'Just what it looks like, my dear,' said Dr Mowbray sensibly. 'The edge of a stone exposed by years of wind and rain. Nothing more.'

But it was something more, as Fanny realised when, temporarily disengaging her hand from her father's, she stepped forward to examine more closely the weird gash in the earth. For – and it hardly even surprised her, this time – as she ran her fingers curiously down the exposed edge of the stone, they encountered a shape they knew well. Bending over, she saw the maze, carved small and deep, as upon a grave.

What did surprise her was that, all that night, waking and sleeping, she seemed to hear music, not a singable tune played on any recognisable instrument, but an echo that chimed and resounded in her head, beautiful, urgent, and yet without meaning. Vaguely, she connected it with that strange, shrivelled grove.

8. Bad News for Hester

AT SCHOOL, the term was rushing on, as summer terms do, in the best June weather anyone could remember for years. Hester's rehearsals had turned into performances, and *The Shoemaker's Holiday*, with Hester Field as Mistress Margery Eyre, had been presented four times in the school hall. Mr Nimmo Lessing, much to Fanny's annoyance, had come uninvited to sit beside the Mowbrays on the evening on which they attended, but, although he had been pleasant enough about Hester's performance in a light, condescending kind of way, he said none of the encouraging things to her parents which he said privately to Hester. Fanny, who knew from Hester's bedtime chat something of the way he had been building up her hopes, found in this something else to dislike about him. She wondered whether Alison knew that he was walking home from school with Hester, every day, and filling her head with notions about the great future awaiting her on the London stage. Part of her wanted to tell her stepmother, because she knew that Nimmo Lessing was dangerous, but loyalty to Hester, who had protected her from Mrs Weber and brought her breakfast in bed, prevented her from saying anything. But she watched the Drama teacher with a bleak, unfriendly eye, and she knew now that she made him at least as uncomfortable as he made her. This pleased her.

When the play was over, Hester suffered awhile from the depression which always follows the end of anything exciting, which has been looked forward to through months of happy preparation. She went about sighing, and making remarks like, 'A week ago tonight was the dress rehearsal,' and, 'Last week at this time, we were making up for the first night.' The rest of the family, who had been through all this before – Dr and Mrs Mowbray several times – put up with it in the knowledge that it was sure to pass, eventually. This time, in fact, it passed more quickly than usual. A succession of new events and developments drove the play out of even Hester's mind, although, for her, one kind of sadness was immediately to be replaced by another.

For, on the way home from school one afternoon, Nimmo Lessing broke the news to Hester that he would not be returning to Millhall High when the new term began in September. Since he had only been there for a few weeks, and term was due to end in another ten days, this came as a complete and very unpleasant surprise to her.

'But why?' she demanded passionately, as soon as she could find her voice. She did not know at that moment whether she was more angry, or grieved, but all at once the sun was shining less brightly, and the green hawthorn leaves, woven through with creamy-pink honeysuckle in the hedge, had gone out of focus. 'Why should you leave? You've only just come. And I thought you liked it here.'

She did not look at him, but she was intensely aware of his lithe young body moving along the pavement at her side, and sensed, rather than saw, the graceful, dismissive movement of his brown hands.

'Oh, I like it well enough,' he said. 'But it isn't my scene – teaching. I can't stand the routine, and let's face it – for every kid of your type, I have sixty in my classes who don't know Shakespeare from the *Beano*. It's boring, and I don't like being bored. Besides – I've got something else coming up.'

Hester waited for a moment, then she asked sniffily, 'And is it something I'm allowed to know about?'

She had shared so many of her secrets with him, it would have given her a crumb of comfort if, now, he had confided one of his to her.

But, 'No,' he said firmly. 'At least, not at the moment. Later, I dare say.'

'When it's time for everyone else to know,' Hester could not help saying bitterly.

They walked in silence along Birkenshaw Gardens, Hester trying to relieve her feelings by slashing savagely at the tops of the privet hedges with the flat of her tennis racquet.

'And when are you going?' she enquired sulkily, as they reached her gate. 'Or am I not allowed to know that, either?'

'Oh, I'm not going for ages,' said Nimmo Lessing, more pleasantly than her manner invited. 'I have business to finish around here before I – well, before I take up another position. I'll be here most of the summer at least, eating nice boiled eggs at Mrs MacPhee's. And if you think about it, Hester dear –' a soft, wheedling tone came into his voice, and he touched her fleetingly on the arm '– there could be some advantages, when we don't have to keep to the teacher-pupil relationship. I mean – you can call me Nimmo, if you like, and perhaps when we're both free during the day, we can see a bit of each other, socially, you know.'

Hester could not trust herself to speak. But she managed to give him a smile of sorts, as she shut the gate. Then she ran up the path, in through the front door, and straight upstairs to her room.

It was obvious, when she came down to the kitchen for supper, that Hester had been crying, but when her mother, surprised and concerned, asked what the matter was, she said that a headache had made her 'feel weepy' – but she was all right now. Mrs Mowbray's further enquiries were cut short by the potato pot's boiling over; by the time she had adjusted the gas and wiped up the starchy water, Fanny had arrived, with the news that Mrs Simpson had seen a Wigan Stoneholdings lorry up on Bieldlaw that afternoon, and surveyors measuring, and men in blue overalls driving white stakes into the hillside.

'I knew it,' said Mrs Mowbray, sitting down heavily on a convenient chair. But she did not have time to expand upon what she knew before her husband arrived, breathless and triumphant, with the gladder tidings that the opposition could stake to their heart's content, but no more. The Civic Amenities Council, he said, had been on to their little game a fortnight ago, and they had managed to get a Court Order, saying that exploratory drilling might not proceed, pending a Public Inquiry.

'And this very morning,' he went on, with the air of a magician pulling a rabbit from a hat, 'we got a letter from the Secretary of State for Scotland, telling us that he has ordered a Public Inquiry – it's to open in Millhall Town Hall on the 2nd of August, at ten o'clock.'

'We'll be on holiday, so we can go,' remarked Fanny to Hester. 'It will be better than a play.'

Hester, who was in a bad mood, said something monosyllabic and discouraging, which came out sounding like, 'Hih,' but Dr Mowbray, glancing with happy relief at Fanny's animated face, said, 'Far better than a play, Fan. I'll be in on the act, which should give you a giggle, for a start.'

'Stuart, this is not funny,' rebuked his wife, as she dumped down a casserole on the table, and lifted the lid. 'It's fishy, to say the least of it. Why has the Secretary of State arranged for the Public Inquiry to be held so quickly? That's what I want to know. I thought that sort of thing took ages.'

'Yes – I suppose it often does. But there was something in the letter about the issue being urgent, because of the implications for local employment. Rory's got our copy, so I can't quote exactly.'

'That must be bad,' said Mrs Mowbray, splashing stew on to plates in a careless fashion.

'Oh, come on, Alison. Cheer up,' begged Dr Mowbray, who had been feeling pleased with himself, and now was not. 'Maybe it hasn't anything to do with employment – politicians have to make the right noises, and try to please as many people as possible. Maybe the Secretary of State believes in conservation, like us. Or maybe this is a slack time of year for civil servants, and they're all twiddling their thumbs at St Andrew's House.'

'Far too many "maybes",' said Mrs Mowbray, lugubriously.

'Well, *anyway*,' said Dr Mowbray, determined to have the last, and hopeful, word, 'we've got all our evidence ready, so I hope the District Council and Mr Joseph What's-his-name are as well prepared. But I doubt it. I can't help feeling that an early Inquiry must help us, rather than them. I'll bet they didn't think anything would happen till the autumn, if at all.'

At this point, he ran out of steam.

Always, in the past, it had been Hester who found these exchanges amusing, and Fanny who scarcely noticed that they were taking place. Tonight, however, for the first time, Hester found herself wishing irritably that Stuart and her mother would both shut up and eat their stew. Fanny, on the other hand, thought for the first time what hilariously funny, but lovable, people they both were.

Just after this, the weather changed dramatically, as if in sympathy with Hester's mood. The sun, which recently had seemed set to do its summer duty indefinitely, disappeared as dark rain clouds whipped across the sky, and the school term ended in a prolonged downpour which washed out the Sports, the Staff *v.* Pupils Cricket Match, the Senior School Picnic and the Cadet Corps Display. Everywhere the flowers were hanging sad, sodden heads, and the tree ring on the summit of Bieldlaw had vanished under a grey wig of mist. On the day when the holidays began, Hester and Fanny, having failed to get on a bus, had to walk home, and arrived soaked to the skin. Nimmo Lessing did not walk with them.

The weather did not bother Fanny; outdoor activities were something she could live without, and she had lived all her life in a part of Scotland where extremes of weather were accepted as normal. Bieldlaw, with its trees rubbed out, reminded her as it never usually did of the rounded Border hills she loved. More and more – although she did not herself notice this – she was remembering former days with her grandmother in a way quite free from bitterness; gradually, as her father had predicted, she was forgetting to feel sad, because her mind was occupied with other concerns. So, as she changed out of her wet things, after the last walk home from school, she did compare the meagre view from the window with the remembered view from her little attic window at Yesterlee, on such a day. A lump of wet hillside and a slice of the boxy house next door seemed even duller when you thought of the leafy crests of beeches and sycamores shimmering through a silver curtain of rain, and beyond them hills dressed in fluttering rags of mist. But instead of brooding over the comparison, Fanny dismissed it from her mind. She was going to spend the afternoon addressing envelopes for her father; the Civic Amenities Council was trying to conduct a last-minute poll, to find out whether most people really were against the quarry proposal. The Public Inquiry was due to open in a fortnight's time, so the addressing of envelopes was a matter of urgency. Hester had refused to help, saying that she didn't give a damn one way or the other.

For it was a fact, and a very alarming one in the view of her mother and stepfather, that Hester had, in ten days, altered in character completely. From a cheerful, sensible girl, interested in everything that was going on, she had changed into a dull, sulky, pouting creature, who mooned idly around the house, returning snappish answers whenever anyone asked kindly what the matter was. Dr and Mrs Mowbray were at their wit's end, and even Fanny, who knew perfectly well that Nimmo Lessing was at the root of the trouble, did not know just how things had gone wrong. Nimmo Lessing had not taught any Junior School classes, and his imminent departure had never been mentioned in front of Fanny. She felt deeply sorry for Hester, but, having once been snarled at savagely for trying to be sympathetic, she did not try again. Instead, she went on waiting for Nimmo Lessing to make another move; she did not fall into the trap of imagining that, because she rarely caught a glimpse of him, his strange interference in her life was over.

Hester's trouble, of course, was partly that Nimmo

Lessing was leaving, and leaving Hester behind him in all the misery and frustration that come from hopes raised, but not fulfilled. But there was something else – something that made the prospect of his departure even harder to bear, although for some people it might have made it easier. This was that, since the day when she had discovered his intention, Hester had scarcely spoken to Nimmo Lessing, except in class, and was convinced that he was avoiding her. If she saw him in the distance, coming down a corridor, she could be sure that before he reached her he would turn abruptly into a cloakroom, or bolt up a flight of stairs. If he came into the dining-room while she and Molly were there, he would pass them with a vague little flutter of his fingers, and go to sit with somebody else. Day after day, Hester had hung about waiting for him after school, humiliating herself in front of Molly, only to endure the chagrin of seeing him cycle off through another gate, in another direction. Eventually, she had picked a quarrel with poor Molly, who had only tried to be comforting, so that now Molly was in the huff, and was going around with another girl in the class, called Natasha Henderson. Hester had been surprised by misery. She had never been unhappy before, and she did not know how to get relief, unless by lashing out at the people who would most have liked to help her. That was why she would not address envelopes to help Stuart, or go to the shops when her mother asked her to, and why she was prepared to spend the whole summer moping in her room, where theatre bills and posters mocked her from the walls. Nimmo Lessing had never even mentioned to her parents the possibility of her going to a Drama School, and she felt despairingly that without his support, her chances of being allowed to go even to an audition were thin indeed.

In this mood of depression, on the first morning of the holidays, Hester noticed something very odd. She would have thought it even odder, perhaps, had she also been in the mood to find it exciting. It was while she was kneeling at the side of the hearth, in the sitting-room, groping under the bookcase for an orange which had fallen from a bowl she was carrying and rolled away, that she noticed something familiar. It was a circular pattern, scratched with a sharp point, on one of the yellow sandstone blocks which formed the end of the fireplace. At first, she could not think where she had seen it before, this intricate, maze-like design within a circle, but then she remembered. It was exactly the same as the one on a silver pendant which Nimmo Lessing wore constantly around his neck. A fortnight ago, Hester would have told everybody, exclaiming and wondering over such a marvellous coincidence, but now she felt that even the mention of his name would choke her, and bring tears to her eyes. So she retrieved the orange, and told no one.

Nor did Fanny tell anyone when she found the same sign on the same stone, as she was sweeping the hearth a couple of days later. She was becoming so accustomed to the sight of it, that now she merely wondered where she would see it next.

9. *A Public Inquiry*

THE PUBLIC Inquiry opened in Millhall Town Hall on 2nd August, as planned, and closed the following day. It was obvious by the end of the first day that the decision was likely to go against the conservationists, and that all the holding of meetings, signing of petitions and conducting of polls had gone for nothing. Despite Dr Mowbray's well-presented evidence concerning the health and safety aspects of quarry development, and the impassioned pleas of several well-known environmentalists who had been summoned for the occasion, the overwhelming need for new jobs in the area made those who spoke against the quarry seem mean and selfish. Mr Pickering, on the other hand, sounded like an angel, concerned only with the welfare of his fellow men. He was a porky, self-important little man with small blue eyes and a harsh, unlovely voice, but angels are known to assume unlikely guises. The Chairman of the District Council who lived at the other end of Millhall, and had always disliked the kind of people who lived at Harts-lawhead, also managed to present himself and his colleagues as compassionate men who cared only for the needs of the people they had been elected to represent. By five o'clock, when the Reporter, Mr Wilcox, adjourned the Inquiry until the following morning, Dr Mowbray, Rory Simpson and their supporters all felt in their bones that their cause was lost.

Fanny, who had waited on at the Town Hall while Alison went out to buy some sausages for supper, pushed her way through the crowd shuffling down the narrow aisles of the hall, and caught up with her father on the steps outside. Silently she slipped her arm through his, and they set off together through streets washed, but not washed clean, by yet another day of rain. It had stopped raining now; the sky was a screen of grey rags, with watery sunshine penetrating the rents, and Fanny thought, not for the first time, what a ghastly place Millhall was. But it no longer angered her that she was there. Not until they had left the town centre behind them, and were walking uphill towards the Lanark Road, with its small stone villas and gardens like miniature public parks, did either of them speak. Then it was Fanny who said sorrowfully, 'It's no use, Dad, is it?' and pressed his arm sympathetically.

Dr Mowbray sighed audibly.

'That's how it seems, love,' he agreed. 'Of course, we can't know for certain what Mr Wilcox is going to recommend to the Secretary of State – he has to submit his report, and the Secretary of State will let us know later on what he decides. But in the light of today's proceedings, I can't help thinking that's a mere formality.' He was silent for a moment, then he went on, 'And the worst of it is, I don't really think I care as much as I should – certainly not as much as poor Alison will think I should. It's so easy to understand the opposite point of view in an affair like this. People round here do need jobs, and you can hardly expect unemployed youngsters at the east end of Millhall to care whether or not affluent folk like us have a quarry on our doorsteps. You heard them, didn't you? They're making us out to be selfish and uncaring – and, God help us, maybe we are.'

'Well, I thought all you said was very true and sensible,' said Fanny loyally. 'It *is* the only green place left in this horrid town, and quarries *are* bad for people's lungs, and it isn't going to provide so very many jobs, is it, Dad?'

'When seventeen per cent of the population can't find work, you can make out a powerful case for a scheme that provides any jobs at all,' replied her father.

'The rabbits will die,' said Fanny gloomily.

They walked on in silence for a while, hearing the birds whistling carelessly in the dripping leaves, while the huge, unsullied green of Bieldlaw towered over the houses on their left hand. As they turned the corner into their own street, Fanny asked, 'What will you do, Dad? About the house, I mean. If the quarry comes.'

Dr Mowbray shook his head.

'I don't know, Frances. I've been thinking about making a move for some time, but it may be I've left it too late. There'll be the most unholy rush to sell houses in the Gardens – we might not be able to get rid of ours at all. We'll see what turns up.'

Her father must be very tired, Fanny thought. This half-hearted Micawberish kind of speech was not like him at all.

It was a dismal evening. Mrs Mowbray, who now maintained that she had never believed they would win, but in reality had never dared to suppose that they would not, was too depressed even to talk, and soon after supper Hester and Fanny slipped away discreetly to their own rooms. Hester had not been present at the Town Hall; she did not even pretend to care whether there was a quarry outside the back door or not, but she wanted to get away from her mother, whom she was infuriating daily by her sloppy, couldn't-care-less attitude to everything. It was an open secret now that Nimmo Lessing's sojourn at Millhall High School was over, but even when she knew what was ailing Hester, Mrs Mowbray found her behaviour no easier to understand. After all, she said crossly to her husband, Hester could not possibly have known him very well, and he was such a tedious young man. So Hester shut herself into her room to mope, and play Patience, and write letters to Nimmo Lessing, which she then tore viciously into shreds before throwing them into the wastepaper basket.

Fanny, also imprisoned, by her own choice, in her little box-like room, got undressed, put on her blue dressing-gown, and curled up on her bed with a book. It was called *Standing Stones and Circles of Great Britain and Ireland*, and she had borrowed it from the Library in Millhall, because there was information in it about the standing stones on Bield-law, and also a photograph. Fanny had been interested to read that the two stones she knew had been part of a circle dating from before 2000 B.C., and frustrated to learn that, while there were a dozen theories, no one seemed sure who had erected them, what had been their function, or what had happened to them. There was the usual vague talk of Druids, which led to a mention of the oak grove on top of the hill; there was also a paragraph referring to the theory of a Professor Larkin, that the missing stones had been taken away around 1600 A.D., and used as building material. Fanny thought of the old house of Birkenshaw, with its reputation for ghosties and ghoulies, and reckoned that Professor Larkin was probably right. Such a house might well have had mysterious stones built into it. There was the one in the sitting-room fireplace, for a start. . . .

Other chapters of the book, too, Fanny found absorbing, but tonight she could not concentrate. Her mind kept wandering back to the scene at the Town Hall, to the rows of hostile, self-interested faces. She heard again the half-hearted patter of applause, mixed with rude heckling, which greeted her father's balanced, sensible speech, and the roars of agreement which had drowned out the last platitudes of the cocky, self-righteous Mr Pickering. It all seemed so unfair – and yet Fanny, like her father, could not help seeing the other point of view. Three factories had closed in Millhall in the last year, and there were men in the town who had given up hope of ever working again. Fanny knew this, because she went to school with their children. Yet it was so sickening that her father, of all people, should be suspected of not caring. He worked so hard, and cared so much. Only he had Alison to consider too, and his daughters. Could it be wrong to put the welfare of your own family first?

Fanny shifted restlessly on the bed, and tried for the third time to read page forty-seven from top to bottom without losing the place. She might have managed it this time, had she not been interrupted ten lines from the bottom by a sharp tap on the door. Almost before she had time to say, 'Come in,' it opened, and Hester entered, looking unpleasant.

'Where's my Dermitex?' she demanded abruptly. 'I lent it to you last week for that ghastly spot you had on your chin. Now I need it –'

'For that ghastly spot you have on your own chin,' said Fanny demurely.

Hester glared at her, then laughed, reluctantly. She sat down heavily on the end of Fanny's bed, and said, 'Sorry, Fan. Don't mind me. I'm just loathesome generally these days.'

Fanny neither agreed with her nor contradicted her, but closed her book and waited to hear what would come next.

'I just can't help it,' Hester went on. 'I feel so miserable. You see, I don't understand. He promised we would meet in the holidays, and that he would speak to Mother and Stuart about a Drama School. Surely they would have listened to him – I mean, he was in *Pericles* and *The Importance of Being Earnest* at the National, for Heaven's sake. I thought everything would work out all right, even if he isn't coming back to school next term. But then he started avoiding me, and I've quarrelled with Molly, and Mr Lessing – well, he's just disappeared, Fanny. I've looked for him everywhere, but either he's gone away or – or he's giving me the slip.'

It all came tumbling out, bitter and angry and desperate, and in a rush of sympathy Fanny blurted out a piece of information which she would almost certainly have kept to herself, had she given herself time to think.

'He hasn't disappeared, Hes. He was there today, at the Town Hall. He was sitting in the row in front of us.'

She did not tell Hester how, at intervals, the old feeling of sick horror had threatened to engulf her, or how, once or twice, the reality of time and place had receded, and the dark shape of the maze stone had begun to whirl before her eyes. She could control these sensations now by an effort of will, but they were warnings to her not to imagine that the dangerousness of the young man had diminished. She suspected that she had some strange effect on him, too, for he kept fidgeting, and half turning round, then looking away again. On the other hand, he might have been sensing the glare of ill will which Alison was constantly directing at the back of his head. One way or another, Fanny had no sooner told Hester about his unexpected presence at the Public Inquiry, than she regretted it. For Hester sat up, with an alert, hungry look in her eyes, and said sharply, 'At the Town Hall? Are you sure, Fan?'

'Yes,' Fanny had to say. 'He was a couple of seats to the right of us, in the row in front. He had that leather coat on, and a black jersey.'

'I'll come tomorrow,' said Hester triumphantly.

The Inquiry reopened at ten o'clock the next morning, and once again it seemed that all Millhall and Hartslawhead had turned out, as to an entertainment. The uncomfortable chairs on the floor of the hall, and the darkly varnished wooden benches in the gallery were crowded with men in working clothes, housewives with bulging shopping bags, old people dressed with shabby propriety, youngsters in denim jeans and studded leather jackets. There was a kind of expectancy in the air, although just what they were expecting would have been hard to say. The Reporter had warned them the previous day that he could not give an on-the-spot decision, and, in any case, both sides believed that today's proceedings were a formality, since the outcome was already decided. Perhaps it was because the great majority of those present wanted the quarry, or perhaps just because in Millhall excitement was rare; at any rate the buzz of conversation was cheerful, while outside the rain ran in long streamers down the grimy windows.

The talking died away gradually as the Reporter, followed by two secretaries, mounted the platform and took his seat at a table. He adjusted his spectacles, and pursed his small red mouth in a way which made him look discerning and properly serious. There was a short bout of coughing and throat-clearing, then, in the following silence, a Mr

Edward Trimble, Secretary of the National Society for the Preservation of Smaller Wildlife, rose to make an impassioned plea on behalf of the Bieldlaw rabbits. The audience lapsed into polite boredom.

Fanny, sitting between Alison and Hester, did not bother to listen. Instead she watched, out of the side of her eye, Hester watching Nimmo Lessing. Once again, he was sitting in the row in front of them, fidgeting even more than he had yesterday. Hester stared at the back of his auburn head with eager concentration, as if by doing so she could will him to turn round and acknowledge her. But she, certainly, had no power over him, and he went on looking straight in front of him while his behind slithered on the slippy seat of his chair, and his fingers strayed restlessly to his collar, his ear, his hair.

The morning proceeded boringly. Some people got restive, and left, but most, like the Mowbrays, decided to stay on till lunch-time, and see the thing through. Expectancy had not been smothered entirely by tedium, and there was a feeling that something might yet happen, and that it would be a pity to miss it. About a quarter to twelve, when Hester had got to the point of planning how she would waylay Nimmo on the way out, and Fanny was wondering how best to avoid him, Mr Wilcox began putting his papers together, and prepared to thank courteously all those who had made their representations so clearly, and, thank God, concisely. He was pleased to have got through this Inquiry so quickly; as often as not, they dragged on for days. He launched into the closing remarks which he had made so many times before, aware of, but not resenting, the general groping for umbrellas and picking up of bags. He himself wanted to catch the twelve twenty-five to Glasgow.

'Before adjourning this Inquiry, I want to assure you that I shall do my best to take all your interests into account in the preparation of my report. All interested parties will have a copy of my preliminary findings as soon as possible. After that, it is, of course, a matter for the Secretary of State –'

The rest of his words were lost in a terrific bellow from the middle of the hall.

'It has nothing to do with the Secretary of State, you

pompous little turnip, and it has nothing to do with you, so shut your mouth and mind your own business.'

The audience put down their bags and umbrellas, and straightened their backs. The Reporter stood with his mouth open, peering over his spectacles, down into the section of the hall where the noise was coming from. He could scarcely believe that he, the representative of the Government, was being interrupted, insulted by a wild young fellow with red hair, who was bawling something that sounded horribly like, 'I know what you're planning to say in your bloody report, you fat gasbag, and so does everyone else here, so don't come the impartial bit with me. I'm warning you, you won't get away with it. There'll never be a quarry on my hill, not ever, do you hear? I've got the power – we – I've got the power to stop it, and we – that is, I'll use it – yes, power – use power –'

The tirade, which had begun with a certain panache, died away into incoherent gaspings. Nimmo Lessing was beside himself with rage, twitching and shaking and waving his fists. A ripple of pleasure ran through the audience. The something which might happen had happened. It had been worth staying on. They all turned about, and nudged each other, and stared at the distraught young man, and at poor Mr Wilcox, bobbing helplessly on the platform.

'Who is it?' they asked, and, 'Must be off his head,' they said, and, 'It's that daft actor fellow that's been teaching at the school.'

Mr Wilcox banged ineffectually on the table, and called shrilly for silence. 'My dear sir,' he tried to say, 'you were given the opportunity to state your opinions. Kindly sit down. This is most irregular.'

Only nobody listened to him.

Then Dr Mowbray got up, and pushed his way along the row to where Nimmo Lessing stood. People made way for him, because they knew who he was. He touched the young man lightly on the arm, and said, 'Mr Lessing, you are unwell. Please sit down.'

Then Nimmo Lessing whipped round, and faced Dr Mowbray. Both Fanny and Hester had a glimpse of his face, flushed and wild-eyed, with his upper lip drawn back from his teeth in what could only be described as a snarl. But then, strangely, the terrible expression changed, as if an air had wafted across it. The angry eyes went blank, the mouth closed, and Nimmo Lessing was staring at Dr Mowbray as if he had never seen him before. Then he turned away, and pushing his way roughly to the end of the row, bolted from the hall. And before her mother could stop her, Hester had run after him.

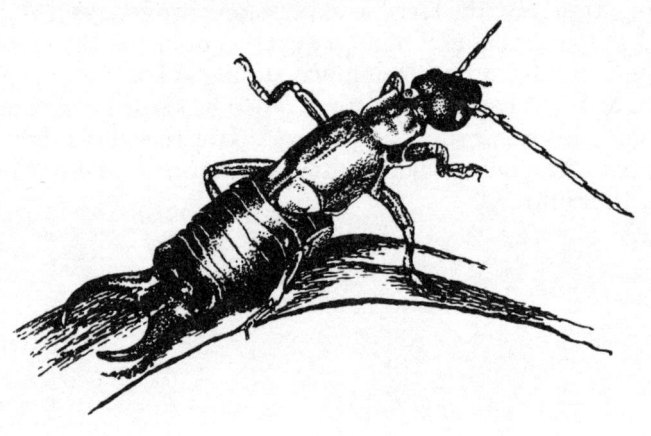

10. Storms

AT NINE o'clock that evening, Fanny was yet again in her own room, because it seemed the safest, as well as the most discreet place to be. Her book was open on the table beside her bed, but she was too exhausted to read. Instead, she was lying flat on her back, staring at the ceiling, and wincing a little whenever Hester's sobs became audible through the thin wall which separated them. For there had been a terrible row, the only terrible row that Fanny had ever witnessed, and although she had not been involved, beyond being told angrily by both combatants to keep out of it, she had been there, and staying out of a row can be almost as tiring as taking part in one.

She had come home from the Town Hall with her father and Alison, whose temper was already beginning to come to the boil, but Hester had not come home. Lunch-time had passed in an atmosphere of furious anxiety, and most of the afternoon. At half past four, Alison had gone out to look for her daughter, and had spent two hours fruitlessly driving round the town in her Mini, peering into the pouring rain for a glimpse of a red waterproof or a leather coat. Hester had eventually returned, brittle and defiant, after eight o'clock, and the row had begun immediately in the kitchen, where the others, without appetite, were trying to swallow haddock pie. It had continued for half an hour in a crescendo of rage, with Alison shouting at Hester, and Hester shouting back at Alison, and Stuart only intervening when things were about to be said which would be neither forgiven nor forgotten. It had all ended with Alison crying in the sitting-room, and Hester crying in her bedroom, having been forbidden absolutely ever to see, communicate with, or mention Nimmo Lessing again.

Fanny and her father washed up together, with misery in their hearts. They had not spoken much, but at one point Fanny had said, 'I wish that Nimmo Lessing had never been born. I can't understand what she sees in him, Dad. He gives me the creeps.'

'There's something not right about him,' Dr Mowbray agreed.

But when Fanny wanted to press him to continue, hoping that, given the right opening, she might at last be able to tell her father about the maze stone, and the reason for her fainting fit, she found that still she could not do so. The words stopped in her throat, and the desire for secrecy once more thwarted her. Following her father's advice, she slipped off upstairs, while he went into the sitting room to comfort his wife.

It did occur to Fanny that Hester might need some comfort too, and she paused for a moment outside her sister's door, on the way to the bathroom. But instinct told her that Hester would rather be left alone, and anyway – she thought despairingly as she went on her way – what could she possibly say about Nimmo Lessing that would be comforting to anyone? So Fanny went off to bed, reflecting, before she fell asleep, that she really must spend a few minutes next day replacing the magic flowers in her velvet bag, as the ones she had were now reduced to a few pale, transparent flakes. The maze stone she had returned some time ago to the pocket of her winter coat; it was not the sort of thing she cared to have constantly about her person.

Breakfast next morning was only slightly less hideous than supper the night before. When Fanny arrived downstairs, her father was skulking behind the newspaper, while Hester and her mother, both pale and heavy-eyed, were having an acrimonious, if subdued, conversation.

'You are not going out, Hester, and that's final. You can do what you like indoors, but you're not going out.'

'I see. So I'm to be kept in prison. That's what you're saying, isn't it?'

'That's what you're saying.'

'And how long is this to go on, may I ask?'

'Till I think it's possible to trust you again.'

'You'll have problems, mother dear. People are prosecuted for keeping other people prisoner, you know. You read about it sometimes in the paper. There was a case recently – some batty old dame in Spain –'

'Oh, hold your tongue, Hester, for Heaven's sake, if you can't say something sensible. As long as Nimmo Lessing – God, what a ridiculous name that is – as long as he's hanging around, you're not going anywhere. I'm sorry, but at the moment I wouldn't trust you as far as I could push you.'

'That's great to know,' said Hester bitterly.

At this point, Dr Mowbray suddenly put down his paper, and looked at them both severely. Like many gentle people, he could be quite alarming when roused, and both Alison and Hester lapsed into silence.

'Now listen, both of you,' said Dr Mowbray firmly. 'This has gone far enough – too far, in fact. We're going to have no more talk of prisons, and not trusting people. There will be no prisoners in this house, and, Alison, if Hester gives us her word that she won't try to see Mr Lessing again, we'll accept her promise, and she will come and go as she pleases. Hester, my dear –' he turned to his stepdaughter with a kindlier look on his face, and put out a hand to her, which she ignored '– surely you know us well enough to realise that all we care about in this matter is your welfare. I haven't asked where you went yesterday, and I'm not going to, but you must try to see things from our point of view. For all I know, Mr Lessing may be a kind and responsible person. But your mother and I feel that he is far too old for you, and, to be honest, that he is not to be trusted. There are far too many unexplained things about him, and that outburst at the Town Hall yesterday was, to put it mildly, odd. All that nonsense about "my hill", and, "we have the power to stop it". I'm sorry to have to say this, Hester, but that's the talk of a person who is seriously disturbed.'

Hester winced visibly, but said nothing.

Dr Mowbray went on, 'So you see, my love, for your own sake, we'd so much rather you kept with friends of your own age, and didn't see him again. Now will you promise me that, if we trust you, you won't go running to see him again? Please, Hester?'

Hester scowled, but eventually answered, 'Yes,' between her teeth.

'Then there's no more to be said. Go out with Fanny, or with Molly and the Simpson boys, and try to forget this man. He's not for you, dearie.'

Alison had gone to the sink, and was expressing her opinion by rattling cutlery and banging pots about. Hester got up silently from the table, and went upstairs. A few minutes later they heard her come down again, and leave the house through the front door. Fanny ate her cornflakes, and wondered how anyone as clever as her father could possibly be so simple; she revised this opinion a little, however, when she heard him urgently asking Alison how soon she could arrange to take Hester away to her sister in Cornwall for the rest of the summer.

'I'll phone today,' replied Alison, wearily. 'No time like the present, to be sure.'

Fanny would also have been interested had she known that, on his way to his morning surgery, Dr Mowbray called in at Mrs MacPhee's Guest House in the Lanark Road, and asked to have a word with Mr Lessing. Mrs MacPhee was sorry; Mr Lessing, she said, had paid his bill and left some time before, the day school broke up, if she remembered rightly. Indeed, she had thought he had left the district, till she saw him making such a fool of himself at the Town Hall yesterday. It had given her quite a turn, she told the doctor. He had seemed such a quiet, pleasant young man, and always so complimentary about Mrs MacPhee's cooking.

Hester could have told Dr Mowbray where Nimmo Lessing was. She had been there with him on the previous afternoon, and she was going there to him again when she left the house after breakfast in the morning. He was camping out – he had been, he told Hester, ever since school finished – in a little green tent in a wood up at Cowden, on the far side of Bieldlaw. No one knew he was there, and she was not to tell anybody. It was to be a secret between the two of them. He had not explained exactly why it was to be a secret, beyond saying that he needed peace to think, and work out ideas for a play he was writing; this might have sounded rather thin to anyone else, but Hester was so thankful to be with him again, under any circumstances, that she accepted it without question, as she did the explanation that he had left Mrs MacPhee's because he was short of cash, and sick of boiled eggs. They had sat huddled in the gloomy little canvas shelter, drinking instant coffee, while the rain pattered on the roof like the feet of a thousand birds, and the rhythmic drip, drip of water from the branches beat on the dank humus floor of the wood outside. Nimmo's face, close to hers, had seemed to Hester haggard and coldly green in the tent's unnatural light; he shivered a lot, and she longed to have him touch her, so that she could put her arms round him, and make him warm. But he hadn't touched her – he never had, except once, at the gate, when he had brushed his fingertips across her sleeve – nor did he even talk to her very much. 'Tomorrow,' he had said. 'Don't ask me things today. I'll tell you tomorrow.'

So they had sat for long hours in silence, while the rain dripped on the roof. At seven o'clock he had taken her back through the wood, and left her where the footpath joined the Lanark Road, about two miles east of Hartslawhead.

'I'll come tomorrow,' she had said. 'You'll still be here, won't you?'

'I'll still be here,' he replied.

Which was why, at ten o'clock the next morning, Hester was scurrying furtively back along the road, trying to avoid the notice of passing motorists by keeping close to the eaves of the wood, which frilled the base of Bieldlaw on this side. Above the wood, the green sward swept up grandly to the ring of trees, sward which presently would be mutilated by the churning wheels of lorries and bulldozers, as access roads to the quarry were sliced out of the hillside. But such things were far from Hester's mind at the moment. Even the fear of being recognised was not uppermost, and she kept to the trees by instinct. In a black hood of rage and resentment, which seemed to shut out all light, she was recalling the things her mother had said to her the night before – that she was selfish and deceitful, that she had been 'making up' to that ghastly man for weeks, while pretending that everything was just as usual, that God alone knew what had been going on behind her parents' backs. Hester felt herself sweating at the memory of these words. They would have been hard enough to bear if they had been true, but her mother had not only jumped to conclusions, but to all the wrong ones. She had not been 'making up' to Nimmo Lessing – he had never given her the chance. He had never even held her hand – this thought pierced Hester with anguish as she turned off the road, and began to stumble up the brambly path under the dripping arch of the trees – yet her own mother had failed to give her the benefit of the doubt. So she deserved anything that was coming to her, thought Hester, with bleak satisfaction. She was sorry she had had to lie to Stuart at breakfast, yet she felt it had been necessary. He and her mother had no right to demand such a promise from her, and, because she was innocent of all they suspected, she should not be bound by it. So she reasoned – and was in no state to consider what was certainly the most important question – whether she could possibly have stayed away from Nimmo Lessing now, even if she had wanted to.

He was waiting for her at the end of the path, wearing a raggy old green pullover under a thin waterproof jerkin. He had denim jeans tucked into Wellington boots, and as he stood smiling down at her, she could tell that he was quite different from the sad, shaken person of yesterday. His handsome brown face was flushed healthily along the cheekbones, and the pucker of anxiety had vanished from his brow. His eyes laughed as he said, 'Have you noticed? It isn't raining! Come and have some coffee.'

There was a kettle boiling on a small primus stove; he spooned coffee into a mug and a tin cup, then poured on water and some powdered milk. They sat on the groundsheet at the entrance of the tent to drink it, feeling the warmth of the long-absent sun on their faces, and watching steam rising from the dense bracken which fenced the little camp site round about.

'I've got sausages for lunch,' said Nimmo, putting out a twig to tease a tiny insect which was weaving its way energetically over the trodden earth at the tent door. 'I popped up to Cowden village and got them first thing. How's that for organisation?'

'Great,' said Hester absently. She had no appetite, and did not want to dwell on the thought of sausages. She paused for a moment, watching the blind antics of the frightened insect, then she said, 'There was a great rumpus when I got home last night.'

Nimmo put down the twig, and let the little creature scuttle away into the grass.

'I thought there would be,' he said quietly. 'I'm sorry. Was it awful?'

'Yes. I was made to promise I wouldn't see you again.'

'That doesn't surprise me either. But here you are.'

'Yes.' Hester raised her eyes, and looked at his face; gaiety had drained out of it, and there was a tired, unhappy look in his eyes which made her hasten to add, 'But I don't care. They had no right to ask me. I've done nothing wrong, and I'd far rather be with you than them. Only –'

'Only what?'

'Only there are some things I've got to know. You see, I don't really know anything about you. I can like you –' she would not be the first to use the word 'love' – but I can't trust you unless you're honest with me. You do see that, don't you?'

'Yes, I do,' he answered gently. 'Ask me whatever you like.'

Hester leaned back against his rolled-up sleeping-bag, and tried to put her thoughts in order.

'Well – first,' she said, 'why wouldn't you speak to me all these weeks? Why did you keep avoiding me? It was horrid. I was so unhappy, and I even quarrelled with Molly over you.'

He smiled a little at this, and said teasingly, 'Doesn't Miss Molly like me any more?'

'No. She said you were an impudent squirt,' Hester told him, and could not understand why this was received with a cackle of delight. 'But why didn't you speak to me?' she insisted. 'It wasn't nice of you.'

'No,' he agreed, 'it wasn't nice of me. But my motives were good, Hester. You see, I suddenly realised that it was very indiscreet of me, a teacher, not only to let myself get so fond of you, but also to encourage you to get fond of me. I mean, I'm twenty-seven, and you're only seventeen.'

Hester was sixteen, but she did not contradict him.

'I felt I was taking unfair advantage of your youth and your inexperience,' he went on. 'I knew I was hurting you a little, at the time, but I did think it better that we should part.'

'And now?' Hester spoke calmly enough, but the words "let myself get so fond of you" chimed like music in her head.

'Now – I think what has to be has to be. Some things are inevitable.'

Why was it that these words, which were what she had longed to hear, sent a slight shiver of fear through Hester? Perhaps because "inevitable" meant that there was no going back. She hurried on to the next question.

'Why didn't you speak to Mother and Stuart about my going to a Drama School, when you said you would?' she asked.

'Ah, that.' He was tracing a curly pattern in front of him on the ground with another twig, tracing it and rubbing it out, then tracing it again. 'Well, I don't know, exactly. Partly, I suppose, because – feeling about you as I did – I didn't want a dishonest conversation with your parents – and partly because I thought I might be better able to help you if I got in touch with some of my drama cronies in London first. Which I have to admit I haven't done so far. I apologise – but I've had a lot on my mind.'

Hester remembered yesterday.

'Bieldlaw,' she said.

'What?'

'Bieldlaw. The quarry. That's what's been on your mind.'

'Yes.'

'Why?' This time he paused for so long, and looked so gloomy that she thought he wasn't going to answer, so she pressed him. 'You should tell me,' she insisted. 'The way you behaved yesterday at the Town Hall – it was very odd, Nimmo, honestly. Stuart said – well, he implied you must be nuts, actually. But I don't think so. I think there's a perfectly good explanation. But you should tell me what it is.'

Nimmo Lessing threw his twig into the bracken, and sighed.

'All right,' he said, 'I'll tell you what I can. I know I lost my temper and made a fool of myself yesterday, and maybe I am nuts, though not in the way your father means. I suppose what he finds queer is that a stranger to this part of the world should care what happens in it, and he'd be right, if I really was a stranger. But I'm not. I've lived elsewhere for most of my life, but I was born at Stoneslap, over Tinto way, and my family had connections going back hundreds of years with the Russells of Birkenshaw, who once owned all the land around here, including the Knowe.'

'The Knowe?'

'What you call Bieldlaw.'

Hester stared at him in astonishment.

'But – you never said anything about this, the night you came to supper,' she said rather reproachfully. 'When Stuart asked you, all you said was that your grandmother, Mrs Gordon –'

Nimmo Lessing dismissed his grandmother with an irritable flutter of his hand.

'Yes, yes,' he said. 'There were Gordons. But the Russells –' a note of pride came into his voice '– the Russells were something special, and it's their property I want to protect. They used to have a house on your side of the Knowe, with the most beautiful garden – a magical place, I remember – that is, the old ones told me about it. It was ruined by vandals and demolished by fools – but I tell you, Hester, they're not going to have the Knowe too.'

Hester did not ask him how he proposed to stop it; doubt and bewilderment were swept aside as suddenly her mind was flooded with the remembrance of something else.

'Nimmo,' she said eagerly, 'I've just remembered. The fireplace in our sitting-room is made from the stones of that old house at Birkenshaw, and do you know, on one of them there's a sign scratched, which is exactly the same as the one on your silver pendant – and the same as the one you've just been scratching on the ground,' she concluded, looking in puzzlement at the smudged marks on the wet red earth.

Hester raised her head, and just for an instant it occurred to her that her companion was afraid. But then his face cleared, and he said eagerly, 'But that's fascinating! Is it really in your sitting-room? It's a kind of secret sign, you know, and its meaning is known to very few people. Only in our family, really.'

'Do you know what it means?'

'Yes.'

'Do tell.'

'Not likely.' He was laughing at her again. 'A monster might appear, and swallow me whole – not to mention your good self. But now, listen,' he added, putting an end to the conversation by scrambling to his feet, 'you're going to slice the onions, and I'm going to get the frying pan heated up, ready for the sausages. And after lunch, you're going home. It won't do for you to be away all day, making your dear family suspicious, now will it?'

11. *A Face from the Past*

ONE MEMBER at least of Hester's dear family was suspicious enough already. All the half-believed, half-rejected fears which had been seething far down in Alison's mind had now come bubbling wildly to the surface, and she genuinely would have preferred locking Hester in the laundry cupboard to running the risk of her meeting Nimmo Lessing again. She had watched her daughter change, in a matter of weeks, from a cheerful, well-adjusted girl into a furtive, sullen creature, and she knew that Nimmo Lessing was at the bottom of it all. She did not give a fig for Hester's promise, so shifty and unreliable had she become.

'Really, one would think she was bewitched,' Alison had said crossly to her husband. She used the word casually, without really considering what it meant; certainly she could never have begun to contemplate the truth, and would have dismissed it as preposterous if she had. The one clear thought in her mind, as she heard Hester leave the house that morning, was that she must get her away from Hartslawhead as quickly as it could possibly be arranged.

So, after she had washed up the breakfast things, assisted

by a silent Fanny, she telephoned her widowed sister Laura, who had a farm near Truro, where she and Hester had spent many happy summers in the past. But alas for hastily laid plans. Her sister would, she said, have loved to have them, but she had only just come home from hospital on crutches, having broken her leg in an accident with the tractor. She was sorry, she assured Alison, but added firmly that she was going to have trouble enough managing the farm, without having visitors in the house as well. She said that she expected to have the plaster removed in about six weeks, and if Alison would like to bring Hester then. . . . Alison did not even try to explain the urgency she felt. She commiserated briefly with her sister, told her to take care of herself, and put down the phone, swearing hard-heartedly under her breath.

Twenty minutes and a cup of strong coffee later, she tried her brother in Sheffield and Stuart's aunt in Sutherland. The one was in Spain on holiday, the other in the throes of moving house. Convinced that the whole world was in league against her, Alison developed a migraine, and retired to bed.

Fanny, meanwhile, had decided that this was a day when one would be wise to make oneself scarce. If Alison was finding it difficult to recognise Hester, Fanny was finding it equally difficult to recognise Alison, and while she did not blame her stepmother for being upset, she was appalled at the way she seemed to be mishandling things. For it seemed perfectly obvious to Fanny that all this screaming and blaming could only drive Hester towards Nimmo Lessing. She at least had no illusions as to whom Hester had gone when she left the house. She admired her father for trying to bring the idea of trust into all this mess, only it was too late for that.

So she had skulked in the bathroom while Alison was doing her telephoning, and, as soon as she heard her come upstairs and go into her own room, she gathered together her purse, her library books and a couple of bars of chocolate to serve as lunch. She put all these in her duffle bag, and crept downstairs to the kitchen, where she added a bottle of lemonade and a plastic cup. Then she set off, walking in the direction of the Municipal Free Library in Millhall. She could spend the morning there quietly, she thought, and in the afternoon she might perhaps go for a ride out to Lanark on the bus.

The same sun that was raising vapour from the bracken where Hester and Nimmo Lessing were sitting at the tent door was shining down on the leafy avenues of Hartslawhead, drying the pavements patchily, and drawing from the gardens all manner of wet, earthy smells. As Hartslawhead merged untidily into Millhall, the gardens became smaller and less luxuriant, while the smells of the earth were smothered by the stronger odours of petrol exhaust and litter. Today, Fanny was too preoccupied to notice either; she crossed Elliesland Street at the traffic lights and walked up Russell Street to the Library, an unlovely Victorian-Gothic building with a sooty statue of Prince Albert over its front door. Fanny skipped up the steps, handed in her books at the desk, and made for the Reference Room, which had in it several large and costly volumes on the lore of herbs. In the main hall, however, with its grey marble floor and bas-relief frieze of local craftsmen and industrial workers, she was diverted by an exhibition. She vaguely remembered seeing a poster advertising it in school, before the end of term, but had paid no attention, as usual. Now, however, although she had no great interest in the history of Millhall and its environs, Fanny thought she might as well have a look round, before going into the Reference Room for the rest of the morning. She bought a cyclostyled catalogue for twopence from the girl at the Information Desk, located Exhibit One, and set off round the stands.

Like most local exhibitions nowadays, this one was well planned and attractively set out. Fanny, as she moved from stand to stand, consulting her catalogue for background information, found herself becoming interested, then more interested still. It was fascinating to examine the tools that men had used in the slate quarries at Cowden a hundred years back, touching to see frail, old fashioned baby clothes and the carved oak cradle in which a little Stewart prince was rocked to sleep at Munday Tower four centuries ago.

But it was not until she came to a fine reconstruction, in

cardboard and plaster of Paris, of the Neolithic stone circle on Bieldlaw, that Fanny's attention was really fixed, and then not by the model itself, but by a huge, blown-up aerial photograph which hung on the wall behind it. For not only did the photograph show, as it was there to do, the darker depressions in the grass where the other stones had stood. It also showed, by a different colouration and slight subsidence in the grass, what that circle of stones had once contained – the familiar outline of the maze, hewn out of the turf, and only much more recently filled in with grass of a different kind. This was something which Fanny knew was not apparent when one was on the ground, and she read eagerly the accompanying information, which drew attention to the base holes, gave detailed measurements, and repeated much of what she already knew from her library book, about possible Druid sun-worshippers, and the removal of the stones. To Fanny's great surprise, there was no mention of the maze pattern on the grass. She stared again in puzzlement at the photograph. Surely it must be as clear to everyone else as it was to her?

At last, some children came up behind her, and their chattering broke her concentration. But as she turned away, she remembered something her history teacher had told her once – that we really know next to nothing about the Druids, and that many of the things with which they are accredited probably had nothing to do with them at all.

Next Fanny looked at the printing press on which the first editions of the *Millhall and District Courier* had been printed in 1820, and actual copies of the paper, behind glass sheets, dating back to that year. She glanced at articles on the Accession of the Prince Regent to the throne as George IV, on the repeal of the Corn Laws in 1846, on the disgraceful conditions in the military hospital at Scutari during the Crimean War. The "Squeak", during its early years, had apparently been less preoccupied with parish-pump affairs than it was today. Parochial doings over the years were represented too, however, in a series of panels which were composed of press-cuttings, old postcards and photographs, and letters written in copperplate handwriting with ink which had turned brown with age. Local residents could learn about the Visit of King Edward VII and Queen Alexandra to Millhall in 1908, the Destruction by Fire of the Alhambra Picture Palace in 1923, and the Victory Celebrations which followed the defeat of the Germans in 1945. But Fanny was not a local resident, and none of these things interested her very much; she thought she would have one last look at the aerial photograph, then make for the Reference Room. But as she turned round, her eye was caught by the unusual title of one of the panels near the door. THE MYSTERY OF THE BANK CLERK WHO DISAPPEARED, she read, and because everyone is intrigued by mystery, she wandered over to examine it. It was then that she got the greatest shock of her life, one which drove the aerial photograph and its revelation right out of her mind. There on the wall, looking straight at her from a faded oval sepia photograph, was a face she knew as well as her own. It was disguised to some extent by a small moustache, and the fact that the hair, parted ridiculously in the centre, was plastered down with oil over the ears. The stiffly starched collar, narrow striped tie and black jacket were unusual too. But there was no mistaking those bright, curiously blank eyes, or that long nose, or the wide mouth, however primly compressed. It might say "William W.G. Maitland" on a card underneath, but it was Nimmo Lessing's face. For the first time, Fanny wondered whether perhaps she was going mad, after all.

She went to the Reference Room, and sat there quietly for a while, till her heart stopped pounding, and the singing stopped in her ears, and her legs felt that they would hold her up again. Then she went back, and forced herself to read the newspaper article, and look at the other pictures pinned to the board around it. It was the story, long forgotten and only now dredged up from the newspaper's dusty files, of William Maitland, aged twenty-two, clerk at the Bank of Scotland in Weaver Street, who, on a Sunday in that ominous summer of 1914, had met with the strangest of fatal accidents. While his fiancée sat drowsing in a gig at the gate of a deserted house, he had vanished from the face of the earth. There were two pictures of the house, which, Fanny instantly realised, was the one whose foundations still lay below the pocket handkerchief lawns in Birkenshaw Gardens. The first was an old brown postcard, captioned "Birkenshaw Ho. by Millhall", which showed a decrepit mansion house of two storeys, solidly built in the style which Fanny, who had learned something of architecture in her Art classes at school, knew to be of the seventeenth century. It had a slated roof, by the time of this photograph badly sagging in the centre, crow-step gables and lots of small, recessed windows. Tacked on to the left hand side of the façade, there was a small round tower, capped with a tiny pointed hat of a roof; even in this old, fading photograph, taken in winter when the garden was desolate and the light poor, you could discern gaps in the slates, and cracks forcing their own way down the tall chimney stacks. The other picture, Fanny thought, as she turned her attention to it, might have been of another place in another world. It was a watercolour painting, in a white mount, of the house and garden in summer, at the height of its prosperity. The door and windows were thrown open to let in the sun which radiated warmth and light over graceful trees, velvet lawns and borders bright with lupins, stocks, carnations, Canterbury bells.

Yesterlee, thought Fanny, with sudden pain. Suppose that Yesterlee should ever meet with such a fate. But she did not have time or inclination to brood, and her attention was caught by some words pencilled on a corner of the picture, just clear of the mount. "F. Haldane, Jun. 1877. Old mansion at Elvanknowe, Lanarks." She compared the pictures carefully to be sure that they were indeed of the same house; she had never heard the name Elvanknowe before.

There was another newspaper cutting. This one told of the shock and grief felt by Mr Maitland's landlady, Mrs Robina Pacey, of 14 Elliesland Street – "Such a quiet, pleasant young gentleman", of the Manager at the Bank, Mr Macdonald – "A nice lad, a conscientious employee", and of his prospective mother-in-law, Mrs Alexander Wotherspoon – "A pleasure to have about the place. Emily is heart-broken".

The report then went on to detail the meagre property found by the police in William's lodgings, some clothing, a tennis racquet, a wallet containing three pounds and a ten shilling note. The only article of any value, it seemed, was a silver key ring, attached to a short silver chain; hanging on the end of the chain was a silver disc, probably very old, embossed with a lovely Celtic design.

Finally, there was an afterword, sad, but probably inevitable. In the bottom right hand corner of the display board, there was an old wedding photograph, showing a grave, rather beautiful young woman in a plain white veil, arm in arm with a bluff, stocky man who seemed to have been squeezed painfully into his stiff wedding clothes. Underneath was a tiny scrap of newspaper, bearing this intimation:

KELSIE - WOTHERSPOON   On Saturday April 15th, 1920, at St Andrew's United Free Church, Millhall, by the Rev. Peter MacCorquedale, M.A., Archibald, elder son of Mr and Mrs Robert Kelsie, of Allanbank Farm, by Roslin, Midlothian, to Emily Ann, only daughter of Mr and Mrs Alexander Wotherspoon, of Sparrowmuir Mains, Cowden, Lanarkshire.

Fanny took a long, astonished last look at the staring, photographed face of William Maitland, Nimmo Lessing.

12. Letters

FANNY EMERGED frowning from the Library into the strong sunlight of a brilliant August day. She had no very clear idea of where she wanted to go, or what she wanted to do; the idea of a leisurely bus ride certainly no longer appealed. It was almost without thinking that she found her way back to Hartslawhead, took the little path along the rear of the houses in Birkenshaw Gardens and climbed the hill to the standing stones. It was very hot, and Fanny was panting like a puppy. Her mind had almost stopped functioning as she crawled into the shady nook under the stone. She lay there for a while, hearing through a red haze the whirring of invisible crickets, feeling the sun burning the backs of her bare legs, which would not fit tidily into the shade. Presently, however, she began to feel better. Under the stones, the grass was still wet, and cooled her burning face; before long she was able to sit up, drink some of her lemonade, and settle herself on her anorak for a good long think.

People didn't disappear. That was the first thing. Or did they? So much had happened recently which before she would have put in the category of things which did not happen, that Fanny was not now quite so sure. This young man with Nimmo Lessing's face – what did anyone know about him? Nothing. They had both come out of nowhere, and one of them had returned into nowhere – except that that was, surely, impossible. He might have gone somewhere strange and exceptional, he might have vanished without trace, but unless one believed – and Fanny did not – that people could disintegrate and be carried away on the air, one really must conclude that he had gone somewhere.

Fanny tried the normal possibilities first. William Maitland had got out at the back of the house, cut along the right-of-way by which she had just come, to the station at Hartslawhead, from where he had taken the train up to Glasgow. Why not? At once Fanny saw that there were two reasons. Firstly, it had said in the newspaper that the doors and windows at the rear of the house were undisturbed, and secondly, he would have been seen and recognised at a quiet country station. Next, she considered the possibility that he had got out through a cellar, perhaps a secret passage – but that was ludicrous too. He would have left tracks in that dusty house – and anyway, was it not far-fetched to suppose that he would have wanted to run away at all, with a beautiful girl waiting for him at the gate, and his wedding planned, and everything apparently happy and hopeful for their life together? And even if, for some reason, he had wanted to get away, why choose such an inconvenient time and place? He could have walked out of 14, Elliesland Street, or the Bank of Scotland, any time he liked. There remained the possibility that he had met with an accident. Again, this seemed unlikely. The Police, according to the news report, had almost taken the empty house apart, and they had – horrible thought – probed every well and dragged every pond over a two mile radius.

Fanny ate some half-melted chocolate, licked her fingers, and listened to the normal daytime sounds of Millhall at her back. She could hear lorries revving up on the hilly Glasgow road, children shouting in the swing park up at Molly's place, a silly little tune tinkling out as an ice cream vendor drove endlessly round the streets on Birkenshaw estate. They were distracting, yet, in a way, a welcome reminder that most of the world wagged on as usual. For the idea which was gradually, confusedly, surfacing in Fanny's mind was so frightening and stupendous that she had to keep contact with the normal world, in case sheer panic should overwhelm her.

Presently, she crawled out of the shelter of the stone, and tried, not very successfully, to trace the pattern of the maze, which she had seen on the aerial photograph at the Library. But she knew it was there. Then she went to the edge of the ridge, and stood looking down at the depressed outline of the old house's foundations in the gardens below. Once a wall had risen, drear and sunless, only a few feet from the hillside, and through that wall, somehow, William Maitland had passed into the unknown. Or on to the hill, Fanny thought. And what was it that connected the house to the hill? The symbol of the maze.

William Maitland – Fanny believed, because rational explanations had failed – had been spirited away from Birkenshaw House, on a stone of which was scratched the maze, and in the garden of which she had found the maze stone. Here beside the standing stones, most ancient of human monuments, a maze had been hewn out of the earth, and she herself had seen another, on the sinister stone slab at the ring of trees. A trail of mazes, in fact, leading from the old house to the place from which, weeks ago, she had seen Nimmo Lessing descend, to enter the Mowbrays' world. Nimmo Lessing, who had William Maitland's face, and a silver maze pendant round his neck. Well, it just might be coincidence, the likeness. But Fanny was filled with a burning desire to discover exactly what was the "Celtic design" on the key-ring fob found in William Maitland's lodgings, in June 1914.

When Fanny got home, having taken a long detour round Hartslawhead to waste yet more time, she found the house quiet. Her father was in his study, writing; she saw his broad back at the desk as she passed the open door. Hester was in the bathroom, washing her hair; you could always tell Hester's hair-washing by the vigour of the splashing. There was no sign of Alison, so she, presumably, was still lying down. Fanny went up to her own room and shut the door. All the time she was undressing and putting on her dressing-gown, and lying on the bed waiting for Hester to come out of the bathroom, she was turning over in her mind the problem of the key fob, asking herself not only what it was, but what had happened to it, where it was now, and how one could possibly find out. It seemed a hopeless task. Nearly seventy years had passed since William Maitland vanished from Birkenshaw, and surely the chance of a tiny key-ring's surviving that length of time was no more than a thousand to one. But on the other hand, Fanny mused, as she made her way along the passage to the bathroom, which Hester had at last vacated, it was mentioned as the only thing of value that the young man had left behind him. If that were so, it really had a better chance of survival than his clothes, or his tennis racquet, for instance.

Fanny ran herself a bath, put in a large quantity of Alison's expensive bath salts, and climbed into the fragrant green water. The pleasure, after the heat and stickiness of the day, was exquisite. She had just settled herself for a long, luxurious soak, with her head on Hester's silly pink bath pillow, when suddenly it occurred to her what was most likely to have happened. William Maitland had had no family that the police could trace, no next-of-kin to whom they could return his pitiful belongings. What was more likely than that William's key-ring, his one valuable possession, would have passed into the keeping of his fiancée – or that she – for all that she had married Mr Kelsie and gone away from Hartslawhead forever – should have kept it for sentimental reasons? Surely she would have kept it; Fanny thought that anyone would. Now, where was it she had gone to live? It had been on the announcement of her wedding. Something bank, by Roslin. That was in Midlothian, where the chapel was. Ashtonbank? No. Altonbank? That was nearer it. Wait a moment. Allanbank. That was it. Allanbank Farm, and Emily's name was Mrs Archibald Kelsie.

Fanny sat up with a swoosh of green water, and grabbed her sponge. Two minutes later she was out of the bath, and two minutes after that back in her bedroom, pulling on a

T-shirt and a clean pair of jeans. Only then did it strike her, with a slight dampening of her enthusiasm, that Emily Wotherspoon had been of age to marry in 1914, and that was nearly seventy years ago. In all probability she was dead long ago, and the Kelsie family dispersed throughout the world. Well, said Fanny to herself, one could only try to find out. Farms did stay in the hands of the same families for generations, sometimes.

Pussyfooting, as she had been all day, she slipped downstairs to the hall, and came back carrying the telephone directory for Edinburgh and the Lothians. She laid the bulky book on her bed, and began to look up names beginning with the letter "k". Kelly, Kelmann, Kelmure, Kelsey, Kelsie. There were about a dozen Kelsies, and Fanny ran her finger carefully down the list. Kelsie, M.J. . . . Kelsie, Peter. . . . Kelsie, Mrs R.A. . . . Kelsie, Robert W., Frmr, Allanbank, Roslin. Roslin 141.

Fanny sat staring at the entry, hardly able to believe her eyes.

It was likely, she thought, that this Robert W. Kelsie would be the son of the couple in the wedding photograph, and would himself be, now, a man in late middle age. The "W" in his name would stand for Wotherspoon. Whether his mother could still be alive or not was uncertain, but at least now there was a chance that Fanny might find out about the key fob, because often such keepsakes were handed down in families. She herself had her mother's locket and Granny's watch and engagement ring. How to approach Mr Kelsie was a delicate question. Fanny felt that she couldn't possibly ring up a complete stranger and launch into such a peculiar tale, ending with a request for such an odd piece of information. It would be too embarrassing, and she would tie herself in knots. She must write him a letter, enclosing a stamp, and simply hope that he would be polite and kind enough to answer.

So there and then she got out her writing pad and a pen, and sat down at her little white desk to write. And after many false starts, and much cross crumpling up of sheets of paper, she produced the following, and thought it would have to do.

>   11, Birkenshaw Gardens,
>   Hartslawhead, ML6 2PG
>   4th August.

Dear Mr Kelsie,
I know this must seem a strange letter, and I hope you won't be angry, and think I am prying into what is not my business, just out of curiosity. I have a good reason for asking, as something very strange is happening here, which I will write and explain to you later, all being well. I found out about you because there is an exhibition on here at Millhall Library, organised by the local paper, which has an account of how Mr William Maitland disappeared in 1914 from a house which used to be where ours is now. It tells that Mr Maitland was engaged to Miss Emily Wotherspoon, who I think must have been your mother. It also says that Mr Maitland left a silver key fob in his lodgings with a Celtic design on it, and it is the key fob I am interested in, because it might help to work out something mysterious. I wonder if you would be kind enough to let me know, if your mother had the key fob and if you ever saw it, exactly what the design was like. Maybe you could do a little drawing of it, please. It could be very important. I enclose a stamp, hoping you will reply, and not just think I am being nosy. I am fifteen years old.
        Yours sincerely,
        Frances Mowbray.

   Fanny folded the paper, dropped a first class stamp into the crease, and addressed the envelope. She was not pleased with the letter, which sounded like fake Sherlock Holmes, and she was afraid that Robert Kelsie would put it straight on to the kitchen fire. But it was a risk she had to take. She could no more tell Robert Kelsie the truth than she could her father, or Alison. She stamped the envelope, and took it down to the pillar box on the main road. It would be lifted at half past five, and might just possibly get to Allanbank Farm tomorrow.

Later that evening, on a sudden impulse, Fanny wrote another letter, and addressed it to the Manager of the National Theatre in London.

'Dear Sir,' she wrote, 'I am a great admirer of the actor Nimmo Lessing, and I am collecting programmes of all the plays he has been in. Could you please send me copies of the programmes for *Pericles* and *The Importance of Being Earnest* which he was in at the National. I enclose £2 to cover the cost of the programmes and postage. I hope it is enough. Yours faithfully, F. Mowbray.'

It was hard to part with two pounds, but she consoled herself with the thought that, should things be as she suspected, the National Theatre would surely send her money back.

13. An Inward Music

TEN DAYS passed, and afterwards Fanny would remember them as a time when action was suspended. It was a period of waiting, when everyone in the house was carefully polite to everyone else, and no confidences were exchanged. They were all waiting for something different, in the short term, and in the long term for something inexpressible, which they knew would alter their lives profoundly.

Fanny was waiting for replies to her letters. For the first time she was discovering the irritation and frustration of waiting for the post to arrive each morning, the lurking in the hall, pretending to be glancing through the newspaper, only to discover that, yet again, all the letters were for other people. Unknown to Fanny, Dr and Mrs Mowbray were also waiting eagerly for letters. Dr Mowbray was expecting an important one from the University in Aberdeen, and his wife was praying for a quick reply to a letter she had written in desperation to her sister Laura, suggesting that perhaps the presence on the farm of an able-bodied sister and willing niece might be a great help to her while she had her leg in plaster. Together, the elder Mowbrays were awaiting the

Report on the proceedings of the Public Inquiry; although they had little hope now that the opening of the quarry could be avoided, they rather wanted the matter settled. But either the post was slow, or no one else was in as great a hurry as they were.

Hester alone did not watch for the postman, or care what he brought. A moderately friendly postcard from Molly, who was on holiday at Scarborough, she tore up and put in the wastepaper basket; a long letter from her former boy-friend, Richard Simpson, who was on a canoe trip in Holland, she read with the detachment of someone receiving a letter from a complete stranger. Two months ago, a scrap of a note from Richard would have delighted her, and she would have carried it around in her pocket for days, but now only Nimmo Lessing was real to her. She ate at home, slept at home, washed and ironed her T-shirts and jeans at home, but even her mother, Stuart and Fanny had become unimportant figures in her life. She went to visit Nimmo Lessing at his camp site every day, and when he told her to, she came home; it was due to his caution and cunning, rather than hers, that she was never away for long, and that Alison, who despite Stuart's intervention, had not scrupled to spy on her, had not yet discovered where the forbidden meetings were taking place.

Into this waiting period, one odd incident intruded, of which only Fanny suspected the significance. On the morning after her visit to the Library, she decided that it would be a good idea to test someone else's reaction to the photograph of William Maitland, and that her father would be the best subject for the experiment. So, at breakfast, she said to him, 'Listen, Dad. There's a super exhibition in the Library, about life in Millhall long ago. I saw it yesterday, and some of it is really fascinating.'

Dr Mowbray looked up from his newspaper, and smiled at her. Thank God, he thought fervently, that Fanny at least was not involved in this wretched business of Hester and the young Drama teacher. It was his one consolation.

'I didn't know you were interested in Millhall, Fanny,' he said.

'Oh, well – a lot of it I'm not,' admitted Fanny. 'But

there's a model of the standing stones on Bieldlaw when there was a whole circle of them, and pictures of that old house and garden you told me about – Birkenshaw, you know.' She forced a lightness into her voice, and went on, 'And guess what – I think I've found out the origin of that story you told me about somebody being murdered and buried under the floor. Only it's even more dramatic. He disappeared – vanished off the face of the earth, I'm telling you. How about that, then?'

Dr Mowbray rolled his eyes ceiling-wards to indicate his opinion of the likelihood of people vanishing off the face of the earth. But as he got up, he said, 'I'd like to have a look at the exhibition, Fanny. Thanks for telling me. In fact, I might just pop in now on my way to the Health Centre – I think this is one of the days when the Library opens early. What about coming with me, Hester? You're not doing anything special this morning, are you?'

Hester said she didn't want to go, but finally went. She had nothing against Stuart, and would still, she reckoned, have plenty of time to get out to Nimmo's camping site by ten, when she had been told to be there.

Fanny was quite excited by the thought of Hester's seeing the photograph too, and spent the day in a fever of curiosity, waiting to hear her reactions, and Dr Mowbray's. But she was disappointed. When the family came together again in the sitting-room at half past five, to watch the television news, and she asked, as nonchalantly as possible, 'What did you think of the exhibition, Dad?' the answer was quite unexpected.

'Well now, that was a funny thing,' Dr Mowbray replied. 'We didn't see it at all, and it's to be closed to the public until further notice. Apparently the Library was broken into during the night, and some of the exhibits stolen.'

'Which exhibits?' demanded Fanny, hoping that her voice did not sound as hoarse and breathless to the others as it did to herself.

'An odd choice, it seems. Nothing valuable – only an aerial photograph of the standing stones, and a few "Squeaks" from before the First World War. And a photograph of your friend, the young man who disappeared.'

Hester, during this time, was also waiting, and although she could not have said for what, she felt that it was something which would change her life totally, and for ever. For the first few days after she and Nimmo Lessing had renewed their friendship outside the Millhall Town Hall, this thought upset her, making her feverish and over-excited. She was also painfully aware of everything relating to their relationship, his physical aloofness, her need to be touched, his evasiveness, her over-enthusiasm in telling him all about herself, her hopes, her dreams, her fears. She knew often that she was being undignified, and felt that she ought to have been more restrained, but she could not help it. All the time she longed to be with him, and the more distant he seemed, the more she longed to draw him close by making him aware of her love. But then something happened which altered Hester. Afterwards she loved Nimmo Lessing just as much, and, if anything, was even more subservient to him, but the pain and strife died out of her, along with the last of her capacity to think for herself. This came about after the day when he asked her to climb Bieldlaw with him.

Hester was being allowed to stay with him for longer than usual that day, because Alison and Fanny had gone to the dentist in Glasgow, and would not be back till half past six. Nimmo was at his most delightful, tender, merry and only mildly teasing; after a lunch of bacon and beans, which Hester had brought, they lay on their fronts on the groundsheet, with their heads at the tent door, listening to the drowsy buzzing of bees in the rosebay willowherb, which had leapt up like fire all around the perimeter of the little clearing. Beyond it was the bracken, and beyond that the wood; only the occasional sound of a car's horn, or the distant thunder of an express on the Carlisle to Glasgow line, were reminders that this secret woodland place had the world for its neighbour. Nimmo had made coffee, and they drank it at their leisure; Hester, delighted by the prospect of a whole afternoon here without fear of detection, wished the moment could last for ever. But suddenly Nimmo got up, rattling his tin cup against the tent pole to rouse her, and said, 'Right then, Lazybones. Up you get. We mustn't waste this lovely afternoon – there's no knowing when we may have another so safe and convenient.'

Hester squirmed reluctantly out of the tent, frowning as the sun struck her head in a burning shaft through a gap in the sycamore branches overhead.

'What are we going to do?' she asked, as she watched him gather up cups and plates, stove and washbasin, and stow them all away inside the tent. His nimble brown fingers zipped up the opening.

'Climb the Knowe, of course,' he replied. 'Doesn't it seem wrong to you that we've never climbed my ancestral hill together?'

Hester did not answer. She did not much want to climb Bieldlaw, to which, for some reason, he always referred by this name she had never heard before. She was a lazy girl physically, as well as a vain one, and the prospect of being blown about on top of a mountain, having her hair disarranged and her nose reddened, did not appeal to her at all. Besides, this reference, as she took it, to the connection between Nimmo and the Russells of Birkenshaw made her uneasy, because it reminded her that she was in love with someone who had never been completely candid with her. She believed that there was some connection between him and the Russells, because of the same design's being on the hearthstone and on his pendant, but whenever she tried to get him to explain further, he became either withdrawn, or irritable.

'Why do you have to keep poking and prying?' he had flared out at her once. 'You're getting to be as sharp as that obnoxious little Fanny.'

So now Hester did not ask, for fear of making him angry again.

It was the last time she would worry over this kind of problem; by the next morning, all anxiety would be ironed out, like creases from her mind. Now, because his word was law to her, she put on her anorak, tightened her shoe-laces, and set off after him through the wood.

It was damp and mossy underfoot, with a decaying smell, and a roof of lace overhead. Hester found it difficult to keep up with Nimmo, who leapt through the bracken with astonishing speed, disappearing behind the boles of trees, re-emerging into sudden streaks of sunlight, laughing in a way that did not include Hester. When she tripped over a crawling bramble, or put her foot accidentally into the concealed trickle of a stream, he did not stretch out a hand to steady her, but all the while she was aware of him beckoning her on. When, eventually, they emerged through the wall of the wood on to green turf under the sun, Hester was panting, dishevelled and close to tears.

Then he was nice as only he could be, and made her sit down for a while with her back against a warm little hummock, and lent her a comb, and contritely helped her to pick pieces of bracken and dried larch twig from her clothes.

'I'm sorry,' he said. 'I forgot your legs weren't as long as mine, and you're not used to this sort of thing. Forgive me.'

Hester said there was nothing to forgive.

'We'll take it easy going up,' he promised. 'It's steeper on this side than it is on the other – you don't have that shelf half-way up. We'll climb a bit, then when you want a break, you tell me.'

Hester nodded gratefully, and they set off, up over the grass dappled with clover, daisies and dog violets. Now Nimmo seemed to notice when she was tired; all the suggestions of stops came from him, and Hester forgot her distress and panic in the wood. She picked daisies and made herself a daisy chain, then she made one for Nimmo, which he hung round his neck on top of his pendant. And this time she thought she understood his laughter, and shared in it. So they climbed, and rested, and climbed, and came to the ring of trees.

Hester was not as imaginative as Fanny, and there seemed nothing sinister to her in the fact that the flowers thinned out, and the summer whirr of invisible insect life died into silence as they approached the summit. Yet even she could not be unaware of the atmosphere in that soundless, windless place. It was the cold she noticed first. The sun shone as brightly as ever, but might have been made of ice, the oak leaves stood motionless on the rheumatic black branches, and there was desolation in the air. She followed Nimmo nervously in among the trees, treading lightly on the poor, flowerless grass, to the gash of earth and stone which had so disturbed Fanny when she came there with her father.

'It's queer,' Hester whispered to Nimmo. One did not speak aloud in that listening grove. 'What is it?'

'A door,' he said softly. 'Only a door, my dear.'

It was then that Hester, too, began to hear music, not with her outward ear, but as an awareness of something very beautiful and strange, which passed into her mind and changed it from within. She did not hear what Fanny had heard; to her, it was the chiming of bells, the calling of flutes, innocent, happy laughter, but mixed up with these lovely sounds was the running of frightened feet, and Hester could hear behind it all the urgent throbbing of drums.

'Do you hear it?' Nimmo's voice asked eagerly at her ear.

'Yes,' she said.

'I'd like you to hear it more clearly,' he said. 'When I ask you, will you come with me?'

'Yes,' she said impatiently, for she wanted to listen to the music, which seemed clear to her now.

But the voice had broken in upon her concentration, and even as she spoke, the inward music faded, leaving only an echo in her mind.

They walked out from the ring of trees on the Birkenshaw side. Before they turned eastward, over the flank of the hill, to descend to the camp site in the wood, Hester saw momentarily the whole world, as it were, stretching away towards the filmy horizon in a vast panorama of houses, factories, cranes and chimneys, roads, railways and shining lochs – the living scenario of modern life, under a dome of shifting sky. And far below her feet, like a dolls' house among other dolls' houses, was her home, in its tiny garden, with washing bobbing on a line. None of it meant anything to her at all.

14. A Quarrel

FANNY HAD had a ghastly time in Glasgow with Alison, and the visit to the dentist accounted for only a tiny fraction of its ghastliness. This was because, in the train going up, Alison had taken the opportunity of interrogating Fanny on the subject of Hester's doings – did Fanny know where Nimmo Lessing was? Did she know where Hester went when she went out of the house? Did she think that Hester was disobeying Alison, and if so, didn't Fanny think that, for Hester's sake, only for Hester's sake, it was her duty to find out where Hester and Nimmo Lessing were meeting, and report back to Alison?

This sort of thing was anathema to Fanny; her answers were at first evasive, then monosyllabic, and finally turned into a reluctant string of hums and haws which irritated Alison almost beyond endurance, the more so because she was smarting under the failure of all her own attempts to find out where Hester was going. She had tracked her to the Swimming Pool, the Café, the Record Shop, but she had never seen a sign of Nimmo Lessing. It seemed that she was fated never to choose the right moment to follow Hester, and Fanny's unwillingness to help was very hard to bear. Long before the train arrived at Central Station, and they stepped down on to the grimy platform, communication had broken down completely between the two, and they spent the rest of the day in the miserable situation of people who have fallen out, but cannot get away from each other.

Moreover, Alison's questions, and evident distress, had rattled Fanny. As she got on and off the sickly-green Glasgow buses, sat in the dentist's ugly waiting-room, and lay on his collapsible chair with her mouth full of cotton wool, she was ill with anxiety and self-reproach. She had no idea where Nimmo Lessing was, although she was quite sure that Hester did, and was seeing him daily; she had no intention of betraying Hester, who trusted her, but it lay very heavily on her conscience that she alone knew of the danger Hester was in, yet she was doing nothing to protect her. The trouble was – what could she do? The truth was so bizarre as to be untellable to any grown-up, and the only chance of alerting her father to the weird possibilities of the affair had disappeared with William Maitland's photograph from the Library. That was the trouble with William Maitland, Fanny reflected, as she spat nasty pink water into the dentist's little basin, he was always disappearing. Now, if only a letter would come from the National Theatre – surely even Hester's faith in Nimmo Lessing would be staggered, if Fanny could prove to her conclusively that her hero was a liar.

The letter was there when they got back. After days and days of hanging about waiting for the post, it had come on the one day when she was not at home. Fanny picked up the envelope quickly to take it up to her room, but not before Alison had caught a glimpse of the words "National Theatre" on the front of it. Behind her, as she climbed the stair, Fanny heard her say peevishly to her husband, 'Don't tell me *she's* going to develop a passion for the stage next – I don't think my nerves would stand it.'

She need not have worried, Fanny thought wryly.

The letter, on impressively headed paper, was polite, and short. The writer, called improbably Godfrey Pepper, was sorry to disappoint Miss Mowbray, but was afraid she must have been misinformed. No actor called Nimmo Lessing had ever worked at the National, and, indeed, Mr Pepper had never heard of Mr Lessing. He was therefore returning her two pounds, with regret that he was unable to help.

None of this came as any surprise to Fanny, who was nevertheless glad to have her two pounds safely back. She knew that it is unwise to send cash through the post, but had been too impatient to wait till she could get to the Post Office for a postal order. She put the notes away carefully in her purse, reflecting that she really must steel herself to talk to Hester later in the evening – always supposing that Hester would even give her a hearing. Fanny reckoned that if she did, there was a fifty-fifty chance that she would believe what she heard; however, an attempt had to be made. Otherwise Fanny would not be able to forgive herself if – she almost said when – something terrible happened.

By the end of the evening, Fanny was forced to admit that these odds were sadly unrealistic. She waited till after supper – a meal at which the atmosphere was made even tenser than usual by Alison's just having opened a terse letter from Laura, stating that the last thing she could cope with at the moment was the ministrations of an able-bodied sister and willing niece. Then she went to Hester's room, with the letter from the National Theatre in her hand. Hester, weary in body and just beginning to become languid because of the echo of the music in her mind, was lying on her bed, amid an appalling clutter of books, magazines, cosmetics, clothes and ornaments, which covered every flat surface in the room, and seemed to rise up the poster-covered walls like silt. It was awful, and Fanny had always hated it, but tonight her mind was on other things.

Hester answered her, 'Can I come in, Hes?' with an unenthusiastic 'If you must.' She watched dully as Fanny picked her way over to the bed, and allowed her bare legs to be heaved to the side, so that there was a space for Fanny to sit down.

'I'm going to stop eating meals here,' Hester remarked. 'It's getting too foul.'

'Yes. It gives me indigestion,' Fanny agreed. She waited

for a moment before adding cautiously, 'Only – they are terribly worried, you know, Hes. I mean, there's this quarry business still hanging over them, and – well, other things.'

'If you mean me, they should mind their own business,' retorted Hester illogically. 'Anyway – what is it you want, Fan? I don't suppose this is a social call.'

She sounded grown-up, in a brittle, unpleasant way, and Fanny quailed inwardly. But there was no going back now.

'I wanted to show you this,' she said.

Hester took the letter from Fanny's hand, and read it with a little fork of a frown between her brows. Through the mist that was beginning to form between her and her world, she realised that Nimmo was under attack, and her wits sharpened.

'I don't understand,' she said, looking at Fanny with suspicious brown eyes. 'At least, I hope I don't understand. What have you been up to, Fanny Mowbray?'

Fanny shifted uncomfortably. This was even more unpleasant than she had anticipated.

'Hes, don't be angry,' she pleaded. 'I did it for you. I hate to have to say this, but – you see, I think there's something very queer about Nimmo Lessing. The man's not right.'

'What on earth do you mean by that?' demanded Hester sharply.

'Well, think of the way he carried on when he came here to supper. And that awful rumpus at the Town Hall – it was weird. He's always given me a funny feeling, and I've never been able to understand why he didn't speak to Dad and Alison about the Drama School business, if he really was an actor, and knew as many people in the Theatre as he said he did. So I decided to find out. I remembered you had told me about him being in plays at the National Theatre, so I wrote and asked for the programmes. This is the letter I got back.'

Hester had been sitting up slowly while Fanny was stammering out her story. Now she looked at her as if she were some particularly nasty biological specimen, and drew up her feet, which had been against Fanny's skirt, as if she feared contamination.

'You rotten, sneaky little pig,' she said.

Fanny's pale face went scarlet, but still she spoke calmly.

'No, Hes,' she replied. 'I haven't sneaked. I could have, but I haven't, and I won't. But I've always thought you were wrong about that man, and I wanted to warn you. You see, I think you may even be in danger. Oh, can't you see,' she concluded vehemently, 'that he's tricked you, and told you a pack of lies about himself? Surely you can't still trust him now?'

When you are in a mess such as Hester was in, the one thing you cannot stand is hearing all your secret fears brought into the open. Suddenly she was in a blaze of anger, and Fanny cowered away from the heat of her.

'Listen, you,' snarled Hester. 'He hasn't told me lies. It's you who are a liar, and a sneak. I suppose you're too stupid to know that actors change their names – Nimmo told me ages ago that he'd had more than one. How do you suppose he got the job at the school if he wasn't a real actor, eh?'

She paused triumphantly, as if this question was unanswerable, and must be the last word. Fanny was hating this more than she had ever hated anything in her life, but she was not going to be intimidated now.

'By telling lies,' she said.

Hester got off the bed, and stood over her.

'Get out of my room,' she commanded. 'Get out, before I dirty my hand slapping your nasty little face. Nimmo said you were obnoxious, and he was right. And after all the trouble I took to be nice to you – you're contemptible, Fanny Mowbray, that's what you are. He isn't a liar, he isn't. You are, and I'll never trust you again as long as I live. He's the only one who understands, the only one.'

Fanny got up, and went out on to the landing with as much dignity as she could muster. Nothing, she thought, as the door slammed behind her, could be worse than this. But she was wrong.

Later that night, as she was getting ready for bed, a note was pushed under her door. Wearily she picked it up, and unfolded the sheet.

'Fan,' it said, in Hester's round, sprawly writing, 'I'm

sorry. I didn't mean any of what I said. I know you wanted to help me, but can't you see it's too late? Please don't tell.'

It was the last straw, and Fanny went crying to bed.

15. *Spy*

THE NEXT morning, Dr Mowbray received the letter he had been waiting for. After he had read it, he announced that he would have to go to Aberdeen the next day to a 'sort of Conference'. He would be away for two nights, and hoped they would all behave themselves nicely till he got back. Fanny noticed that there was a pleased note in her father's voice, and that Alison looked a little more cheerful when she heard the news; she wondered vaguely if there was something in the wind, but did not spend time speculating. For she too had got a letter, with an Edinburgh post mark, which was now in her jersey pocket awaiting a convenient and private reading time. This did not come till after the breakfast dishes were washed, and she and Hester had done their holiday chores; Hester, looking dazed and heavy-eyed as one does after a sleepless night, then departed with her mother to buy shoes and new sports gear for the approaching school term, while Fanny went out to the bench behind the greenhouse to read her letter.

Now that it had actually arrived, she was afraid to open it. Ever since she had seen the photograph of William Maitland in the exhibition at the Library, doubts had gradually been crowding in upon her. Could she have imagined the likeness between William Maitland and Nimmo Lessing? Was it possible that, just because she had Nimmo Lessing 'on the brain', as Hester would say, she had seen similarity where none existed? After all, no one else from the house had seen the photograph, so there was no second opinion to back hers up. But then, some one *had* taken the trouble to break into the Library to remove the photograph, which would have been a very peculiar theft, unless that someone didn't want the photograph to be recognised. . . . Still, only a description of William Maitland's key fob would prove anything conclusively to Fanny's mind, and, so afraid was she of disappointment, she sat on the bench for ages, turning the pale blue envelope over and over in her hands, before she found courage to open it. The letter consisted of two sheets of lined paper, written over in thick black ink. The writing was rather shaky, but well-formed in a very old-fashioned way, and as Fanny read she gradually stiffened into rapt attention.

'Dear Miss Mowbray,' the writer had written, 'My grandson, with whom I live here at Allanbank, has given me the letter you sent him, because he says I am the best person to answer it, as perhaps I am. Yes, after all these years, I still have poor William's key-ring, it is here beside me on the table. The fob in which you express interest is about the size of a florin, what nowadays you call a ten pence piece. On one side it is blank, and on the other there is a raised design, a kind of maze is the best way to describe it, with spiral markings which you can trace to a point in the centre. I don't know what it means, but a cousin of my late husband, who was a history teacher, once told me that it was of great antiquity and that the maze pattern was supposed to have magical significance. Although I don't suppose you young ones believe in that sort of thing nowadays. He thought I should sell it, but I could not do that, it being all of poor William's that I have.

'My dear, I wonder if perhaps you have discovered

something which could throw light on what happened to my William long ago. If you have I would be obliged if you would let me know, such an old mystery as it is, it still distresses me sometimes at night if I cannot sleep, with the music I heard then. He was a handsome fellow but never told me much about himself.

'Excuse bad writing. I am eighty-nine now and my sight is not what it was, although I keep well.

'I hope I hear from you again.
              'Yours sincerely,
                    Emily Kelsie.'

Fanny read the letter through several times, then she folded it up carefully and put it away in her pocket. Her first thought was that when all the mystery was at an end, she would go to see this nice old lady in Roslin, and tell her all she knew. How terrible to lie awake at night, worrying over something that had passed into history seventy years ago. And hearing that music which she too had heard, and which still, occasionally, sounded its faint, sombre echo in her mind. But meantime, Fanny knew that looking after Hester must be her first concern, because Hester was in thrall to something so extraordinary that Fanny's mind literally went dark at the thought of it. Yet one stupendous thing was now clear enough. Whoever William Maitland had been – and certainly he had not been the nice young man from the Bank whom his contemporaries thought they knew – and wherever he had gone, he had come back, and was on the loose again, calling himself Nimmo Lessing. One could not help thinking that Emily Wotherspoon had had a lucky escape, and now Hester – Fanny shivered, and dared not finish the thought. The terrible thing was that, lacking the evidence of the photograph, still no one would ever believe a word of her story, so the guarding of Hester was going to fall entirely to her. Now it really was Fanny Mowbray against Nimmo Lessing, and Fanny wondered, sitting there cold on the bench in the sunshine, how many magic flowers you needed to win a battle like that.

Meantime, however, she must decide what she was going to do. Last night's experience had proved that there was no point in appealing directly to Hester, nor would it be feasible to kidnap her, and keep her tied up till Nimmo Lessing obligingly took himself off elsewhere. The main thing must be to find out where Hester was going to meet Nimmo Lessing – sneaky or not, it was something Fanny had to know. Indeed, she had to know where Hester was every minute of every day, from now on, so that, if necessary, help could be summoned in time of great need. Fanny decided that the only way to discover the meeting place was to follow Hester, but that, fortunately, was something which could be shelved till the afternoon. Alison's and Hester's shopping trip would occupy the rest of the morning. She therefore had two free hours, and she determined to spend them in trying to find out something which puzzled her – who were these Russells, from whose house a person could vanish, and who had on their wall the recurring magical sign? There was a Local History section in the Reference Room at the Library, and she would go down there now; it seemed likely that there would be some information about a family of local importance. So Fanny got her bicycle out of the cellar, and cycled down to Millhall.

The Library was almost deserted. Fanny went across the hall, past the closed Exhibition which was concealed by huffy white screens, and into the Reference Room, where in the past she had spent many contented hours with the herb books. After some peering at the shelves, she found a large, leather-bound tome entitled *Who Was Who in Lanarkshire 1500-1900*, and staggered with it to a reading-desk. Finding that the entries were in alphabetical order, she looked up 'R', and was pleased to find 'Russell of Birkenshaw' under a drawing of the family coat-of-arms. Feeling with her bottom for the edge of the chair, Fanny began to read eagerly down the narrow column of tiny print.

To begin with, it seemed that she was not going to come upon anything peculiar. The first Russell of any note had been a sea-captain turned merchant, who had bought land and built the house at Birkenshaw, marrying a Lady Susannah Oliver in 1652. Their descendants seemed to have been a prosperous, dull lot, lawyers, ministers, two Members of

Parliament. Not till 1786 did anything untoward enter the records. But in that year – here Fanny felt her whole body stiffen – the wife of Sir Oliver Russell, his bride of but a few months, had disappeared from Birkenshaw. It was assumed in the family that the lady had eloped with the local apothecary, Mr Kidd, who had left the parish at the same time, but nothing further was ever heard of her, and her departure had given rise to a persistent local legend that she had been removed by the fairies – a superstition strengthened by the proximity of the house to the mound known as Elvanknowe. In the nineteenth century, the fortunes of the family had declined, and the line had died out with the death of Miss Victoria Russell, the noted occultist and traveller, in 1897.

Fanny closed the book and sat back in her chair, letting out her breath in a low, astonished whistle.

There was no time to brood, however. Through a lull in the blessed, normal traffic noise outside, she heard the clock of St Stephen's church striking twelve, and realised that she must hurry home. Lunch was at twelve thirty, and after that, she must turn her attention to tracking Hester. As she cycled back up to Hartslawhead, she tried not to dwell on what she had just read, but to work out what she was going to do in the afternoon. She had no experience of stalking people, and she wondered whether disguise would be a good idea. So when she got home, she went upstairs and tried on a variety of garments, an old raincoat and headscarf, a long skirt, fur jacket and hat which she had worn as a Posh Lady in a class-room play, a huge green fishing jacket and sou'wester of her father's. The effect was so ludicrous that she abandoned the idea; the last thing she wanted, she observed grimly to her reflection in the mirror, was to have Hester come up to her in Weaver Street and say, irritably no doubt, 'For glory's sake, Fanny, what on earth are you doing guyed up like that?' She put the clothes back in the cupboards where she had found them, and decided that, after all, she must trust to her thinness and nimbleness of foot to keep herself out of sight when Hester seemed to be facing in her direction. She took off her scarlet jersey, and put on one as green as leaves, but she did not choose the colour deliberately, as she had not thought of going into the country. Then she went downstairs, ate soup and cheese, and lounged in the sitting-room until she heard Hester go out.

It was a long way from Hartslawhead to the Cowden Woods, and Fanny had a most panicky journey. It was easy enough to avoid Hester's notice as long as they were still in the streets; she had tied a dark scarf over her bright hair, and it was easy enough to stop and look in a shop window, or slide into a doorway, if she sensed that Hester was about to look back. Once they were out in the country, on a road with only a grass verge for pavement, and a ditch between it and the outmost rank of trees, it was much more difficult. Time and again, as Hester glanced nervously over her shoulder, Fanny had to freeze against a tree, or drop hastily into the grass, with her heart thumping against her ribs. For she knew that if Hester saw her, it was all over; she would never stand being spied upon. Nobody would. But luck seemed to be on Fanny's side, and she was not spotted. When Hester got to the turning into the wood, she was able to take a parallel path through high bracken, and find a fallen tree trunk behind which she could lie hidden, and look down on the little camp site in the clearing.

'Please God, don't let me sneeze,' she prayed fervently.

Nimmo Lessing was sitting at the tent door, whittling a piece of wood with a knife. In his short-sleeved shirt and old trousers, he looked exactly like any ordinary young man on a camping trip. Fanny was not close enough to hear low-pitched voices distinctly, but she saw, as one watching a mime, Hester run up to him, kneel down beside him, and speak to him with a kind of dog-like eagerness which Fanny found both pathetic and distasteful. She had to lie there in the bracken, being tickled by grass and explored by insects, watching Hester making coffee on a little primus stove, and bringing out chocolate biscuits from the pocket of her anorak. Fanny saw them eat the biscuits and drink the coffee, sitting side by side on a rug at the tent door; what struck her most forcibly, apart from Hester's fawning manner, was that Nimmo Lessing scarcely spoke to Hester.

There was no laughter, no shared joy, none of the caressing which Fanny would have found horribly embarrassing, but would at least have understood. When she thought of Alison's suspicions, and the way she had spoken to Hester on that dreadful evening after the rumpus at the Town Hall, her heart ached for Hester, yet she could not help feeling that if Alison had been right, Hester's love for this fearful young man would, at least, have been less puzzling. How could anyone fall in love with such an icy, ungracious creature? What Fanny did not know was that he had not been icy, or ungracious, before he had finally made Hester his own at the ring of trees.

Not long after the coffee was finished, Nimmo Lessing told Hester to go, and she got up obediently, fastening up her anorak. He came with her along the path, passing within a couple of feet of Fanny, who held her breath and prayed again not to sneeze. Now she could hear their voices, and she did not like what she heard. It seemed like the continuation of a conversation begun when they were out of earshot.

Hester said, 'Nimmo, when?' and he replied in his smooth, accentless voice, 'Soon.'

'But how soon?'

'I'll let you know, when the time comes. Unless, of course, anything happens in the meantime which you think I ought to know. But it had better be important, Hester – I don't want you coming out here again, unless you have something vital to tell me. Remember – I might be angry, and you don't want that, do you?'

'But Nimmo –'

'Just do as I say, Hester. Surely you realise by this time that I always know best?'

Fanny thought that if she had had a knife handy, she would have stood up there and then, and run him through.

She knew that she would have to lie low long enough, at least, to allow Hester to walk part of the way home, and also that she must be very careful not to be spotted by Nimmo Lessing, who – she thought grimly – did have a knife, and might run her through. So, as Hester's forlorn footsteps receded into the distance, she lay still, watching Nimmo

Lessing walk back to the tent and potter about, rinsing the coffee cups and folding up the rug. She saw him pull a jersey from the interior of the tent and put it on, then he stood up with his face in her direction, and took off the silver pendant which he wore constantly around his neck. For a scared moment, Fanny thought he had located her, and was going to use the pendant to put a spell on her, but it was not so. Looking up into the sun, and holding the pendant in the cup of his hands, he used the burnished underside of the disc as a mirror, shifting it this way and that until the sun's beam caught it, making a light that was as hard as a diamond, and as quick and bright. And high up on Bieldlaw, from the edge of the ring of trees, there came an answering diamond flash, just one. Nimmo Lessing put the pendant chain around his neck again, and began to walk slowly up the woodland path that led to the hill.

When Fanny was out on the road again, she could see him, far away on the hillside, yet larger surely than he should have been from that distance, striding up without pause for breath over the grass. There was something suddenly magnificent about the tall, upright young figure under the sun; it seemed to radiate pride, and beauty and majesty such as Fanny had never associated with Nimmo Lessing before. From far down in her memory, some lines came singing, lines she had learned long ago, in her childhood at Yesterlee:

> 'How beautiful they are,
> The lordly ones
> Who dwell in the hills,
> In the hollow hills.'

'Oh, glory,' said Fanny inadequately. 'Oh, glory be.'

16. At the Cowden Woods

THINGS HAPPENED very quickly after that.

Next morning, Dr Mowbray departed on the train to Glasgow, *en route* for Aberdeen; he was looking very spruce in his best suit, and Fanny, who went to the station to see him off, could not resist asking him since when going for an interview had been renamed going to a sort of Conference. Dr Mowbray looked so crestfallen that Fanny burst out laughing, although she was not really in a laughing mood.

'It's a University job,' he told her. 'Chair of Community Medicine, and I think I have a good chance of getting it. Would you like to live in Aberdeen, Fanny?'

'It's nice,' Fanny said, remembering sharp grey buildings under a cool sky, and a long pewter line of sea. 'I was there with Granny once, on a sort of holiday.'

Dr Mowbray laughed, and kissed her quickly as the dark green diesel pulled in at the platform.

'Take care till I get back,' he said.

While her husband was away, Alison, who was feeling remorse, did her best to give Hester and Fanny a pleasant time, taking them on outings, including one to Edinburgh, to see a matinée performance of *Giselle*. It was a way, too, of keeping Hester under her eye. To Fanny, it was some relief to get away from Hartslawhead, although there was something unreal about going through the normal routines of sightseeing and eating out, under the circumstances. Still, she made an effort to appear bright and interested, because she knew that Alison was trying to make amends. Hester, who had drifted into a kind of waking dream from which one voice alone could rouse her, was docile and pleasant enough to convince her anxious mother that the worst was over. If only Stuart got the Aberdeen job, and she got Hester away from Hartslawhead soon, everything would be all right, Alison thought. Afterwards, Hester could not remember where she had been, or what she had seen. All that was clear in her mind was Nimmo's instruction – she was to wait till he called her, unless anything unexpected happened. If it did, she was to go to him.

The unexpected, as far as she was concerned, happened the next day, which was a Friday.

Dr Mowbray arrived back on the 12.15, bringing the news that he had been appointed Professor of Community Medicine at Aberdeen, so the family would be moving north in time for the University term in October. Meanwhile, he said, the girls had better start packing, as he had rented a cottage at nearby Cove Bay for the rest of the summer. They would be going there with Alison on Monday, to combine a seaside holiday with the business of seeing about schools and uniforms; he would join them when his leave began in a fortnight's time, so that house-hunting could begin in earnest.

Since Hester was the only person in the house to whom this news came as a complete surprise, her stunned expression passed without much comment. Dr Mowbray patted her on the shoulder and said kindly, 'Sorry, Hes. I know it's a bit of a shock, but you're an adaptable lass, as you've shown before. You'll soon get used to the idea.'

'What will happen to this house, Dad, if the quarry does open up?' Fanny asked, as they sat in the sitting-room sipping the champagne which had been brought forth at the double by a euphoric Alison. 'You'll have trouble selling it, won't you?'

'Apparently not, Fanny,' he said. 'I actually have an interested would-be purchaser – eager, I might say.'

'Who?' cried Fanny, in astonishment.

'Mr Joseph Pickering, no less. He wants a house in Birkenshaw Gardens for his quarry manager, and I have a house to sell.'

Fanny was silent for a moment, while she thought this over. Then she said slowly, 'So we're well out of it. But what about all the other poor folk who can't get posh jobs in Aberdeen, or sell their houses to Mr Pickering?'

Dr Mowbray frowned, and Fanny thought she was in for a sharp retort. But all he said was, 'Look, Fan. I've thought of all that, too, and if our staying was likely to help any of them, I might have taken another decision. But it isn't. If the quarry comes, they'll just have to do their best for their families, as I have for mine. I've given nearly twenty years of my life to this town. I did what I could to help my neighbours when this affair was first mooted, and there I have to leave it. Life isn't fair, Fanny.'

'There isn't going to be a quarry,' said Hester, as one making a statement of fact.

But the others had fallen to talking about Aberdeen, and nobody seemed to hear her.

While they were having lunch, Rory Simpson came with a copy of the Report which they had all been waiting for. It had been sent to him, as Chairman of the Civic Amenities Council. As expected, Mr Wilcox had recommended to the Secretary of State that the quarry project should go ahead, subject to certain restrictions on the times when blasting might take place, and the number of lorries which might use the access road through Birkenshaw Estate on any one day. This, presumably, was what he had meant by taking everyone's interests into account.

'He was a feeble little specimen,' said Rory bitterly. 'That daft teacher chap wasn't far out. Ah well, folks – it's everyone for himself now.'

It seemed an indelicate moment to tell him that the Mowbrays had already made provision for themselves.

Hester went through the afternoon like one in a trance. She knew that she must get out to the Cowden Woods with all the news as soon as possible, but that could not be managed till evening; since Dr Mowbray had the rest of the day off, they were all going swimming in the afternoon. This did not chafe Hester as it might have done; she realised that evening was better, since, after an early supper, Dr and Mrs Mowbray were going out to the cinema, in Millhall. They thought there was nothing to worry about now; Hester might meet Nimmo Lessing to say goodbye, but on Monday she would be two hundred miles from Hartslawhead.

Fanny did not share their optimism, although she too miscalculated. She knew that Hester would make her way out to Cowden that evening, and she intended to be there too, within earshot, because she wanted to know what Nimmo Lessing's last orders would be. She had no doubt now that, at some point during the week-end, he would try to make off with Hester, and she wanted to know when, so that she could tell her father, and have Hester restrained. The time was past for feeling squeamish about loyalty, and telling tales; Hester was in terrible danger, and Fanny thought that only by telling her father could she now save her, from Nimmo Lessing, and from herself. It seemed unnecessary to try to tell the whole story – surely if she said she had proof that Hester was going to be abducted, that would be enough. Only she must know where and when the abduction was to take place.

It was far too dangerous, Fanny felt, to risk following Hester again by the road. Only by good luck had she not been spotted the last time, and now that she knew where Hester was going, there was no need. Instead, she would see Hester off, then cut over the flank of Bieldlaw, coming down through the trees above the camping site – a route which she supposed Hester had never taken because her mother would have seen her from the kitchen window. Fanny hoped fervently that she would not think of taking it tonight. She wanted to be there, hidden in the bracken, before Hester arrived at the camping site.

Later in the afternoon, when they came back from the

swimming pool, Fanny made the only preparation she could. Going out into the garden, she picked up some fresh sprigs of the herbs that turn away evil: betony, St John's wort, herb bennet – wood avens, they call it in the country – and made a chain of them, which she put round her neck under her green jersey. It seemed a paltry protection, in the face of such stupendous danger, but once before it had given Fanny courage to stand up to Nimmo Lessing. Courage, and a cool head, were what she needed now.

It was as a second thought, and without really knowing why, that she put the maze stone into her pocket, before going downstairs to supper.

Hester watched from the sitting-room window as her stepfather backed the car out of the garage, and into the road. Her mother got in, and they drove away, laughing and talking cheerfully. Hester heard the sound of the engine dying away down the street, and wondered if she had seen these people for the last time. It was not a thought which gave her pain or pleasure; the music in her head had taken away all her power to feel. She must go to Nimmo; he would know what to do. Taking nothing with her, she left the house, and set off for the Cowden Woods. Fanny need not have worried about her taking another road. She was incapable of taking any new decison, and could only do what she had done before.

It was half past eight when she reached the woods. Already the summer nights were shortening towards autumn, and although the sky was still clear, it had gone an ashy colour. Through the gaps in the trees could be seen a few weak stars, and a hard, high-riding, small white moon. Hester ran quietly down the path through the rusting bracken; at least, she thought she was being quiet. In fact, Nimmo Lessing, sitting waiting for her on the edge of the clearing, had heard her every step since she left the road. He stood up as she approached, and watched her with a strange little smile playing around his wide mouth. He was dressed in grey, and glimmered in the shadowy glade.

'I was expecting you,' he said.

Hester's mind seemed to clear a little at the sight of him,

and she ran forward to him, saying eagerly, 'Nimmo, you're not angry, are you? You said I could come, if I had something important to tell you. Well, I have. Mr Simpson got a letter today from the Scottish Office, and they're going ahead with the quarry.'

'Now tell me something I don't know,' he replied, coldly teasing.

Hester did not notice his tone.

'Stuart has got a job in Aberdeen,' she told him, 'so we're leaving Hartslawhead. Mother and Fanny and I are going on Monday in the Fiat, and Stuart's coming on in the Mini in two weeks' time. At least – that's the plan.'

The cool expression of Nimmo Lessing's eyes did not waver, but his straight dark eyebrows lifted, and his mouth pursed into a soundless whistle.

'Now, that I didn't know,' he said. 'What a good little girl to come and tell me. So it must be tonight, mustn't it?'

It was then that Hester noticed that the little tent had gone, leaving only a blanched patch on the grass to show that anything so normal had stood there. She looked up uncertainly at Nimmo Lessing, who now came forward from the trees, and his clothing seemed to her like grey silk, his hair like withered leaves.

'Tonight?' she faltered.

'Tonight, you and I must take the road together, my dear,' he replied.

'What road?' Hester asked the question, but as she asked it, she knew. Once she had dreamed of taking the road to London with a handsome young actor, but he was far, far from this fey creature who towered above her, his face clear and pitiless among all the shadows. The music was dying and falling in her head, and as her mind sharpened, she realised that she was in a trap. As she started back, he stepped forward and grasped her wrist. It was like a fetter going on, and for the first time Hester knew why he always avoided touching people if he could. His touch was not like flesh.

'No,' she gasped, beginning to struggle. 'I won't come with you, I won't. Nimmo, please – if ever you loved me, let me go home.'

If she thought that appeal would work, she was quickly disillusioned. Nimmo Lessing – it was one of many names he had had – laughed mirthlessly.

'Love you?' he said. 'I never loved you, silly girl. My kind are not supposed to love, though I did once, and out of pity left her under the sun, when my time ran out. Sorely I suffered for that foolishness, and I shall not make the same mistake again. I never loved you. I'd rather have had the other one, but she resisted me.'

Hester fluttered helplessly in his steely grasp. All the past, warm life with her parents, and Fanny, and Richard, and Molly, rose before the eye of her memory, and she longed for its return with a passion which almost broke her heart.

'Then why me?' she moaned. 'Why me?'

He was impatient now.

'Because it is the time, seven years times ten, and you – for want of a better – are my chosen. Did you not long to be my bride? Then come.'

He turned abruptly, and dragging Hester by the wrist, moved up the path toward the hill. Fanny crept out of the bracken and followed them. There was nothing else she could do. But chill fingers touched her heart.

17. *The Lordly Ones*

IT WAS, as he had said, a door, and now it stood open, a gaping mouth in the hillside, and within was a tunnel, filled with a grey, sourceless light. Once over the stone threshold, with the light of her own world behind her, Hester's terror mercifully eased, as again she heard the strange music of the hill, rising, falling, beating, chiming, but mixed through it now the soft padding of resolute, though frightened feet. As she lapsed deeper and deeper into trance, the cold grip on her wrist loosened, until she could scarcely feel the fingers there; she was being drawn, rather than dragged, down into the underground passages of faery Elvanknowe.

Hester would never know how long that journey took, with the wild, altered figure of Nimmo Lessing at her side. Grey dreams flitted past her on the walls, pale knights riding, wild beasts prowling, waves beating on a broken shore, under a cold moon. Sometimes her feet were heavy, as though she was wading through deep water, and sometimes invisible briars scratched her face, and caught in her dishevelled hair. But she felt no pain, as she stepped to the music that throbbed and rang, urgent and lovely beyond any music on earth. At last – it might have been after minutes, or hours, or days – the tunnel seemed to open out into a vast, circular stone chamber, with a domed roof in drifting shadow far above. It was lit by a thousand cold, unflickering candles, held by people, rank upon rank, all in grey, with secret faces and garlands of withered leaves upon their heads. But they were like the dreams which had passed Hester on the walls; they were tall and lordly, and perhaps they had been beautiful once, but now they were without substance, withered like their garlands and as dry as death. Some of them had been human, and now Hester was to join them. The music had thinned into silence, and a blade of despair pierced Hester's heart. But she could not cry out.

Now her escort was leading her to the centre of the chamber. As they moved, one of the figures seemed to detach itself from the rest, and stepped towards them. Hester kept her eyes down, afraid to meet the stern, colourless gaze. But she was aware that the figure was holding something in its hand, and as it raised its ashen arm she saw that it was an apple, bright and golden, shining in that awful place. A smell of warmth, light and summer flew out from it, and the whole chamber was filled by a rustling, longing sigh. But Hester knew that the apple was for her alone. It glowed enticingly on the dry palm that offered it, and because her mouth was dry as dust, she wanted it desperately. But some instinct held her back.

'Eat,' commanded the creature who had been Nimmo Lessing. And again, as she hesitated, 'Eat.'

But just as her fingers closed round the golden fruit, someone stepped forward, and struck the apple from her hand.

'No,' said a voice she knew. 'At least we know better than to eat in this place. You come with me, Hester. We're going home.'

They were brave words from a despairing heart, but Hester felt something like joy as she turned and clutched at Fanny, and felt Fanny's thin arm go round her waist. Watched in silence by the motionless grey throng, they backed slowly towards the entrance to the tunnel. But just as they reached it, like dry leaves lifted by a sudden wind, the grey figures rose, and surged hissing towards them over the wide stone floor. The thought of being engulfed by them was unbearable, and Fanny, terrified, reached for the only weapon she had. She took the maze stone out of her pocket, and hurled it among them with all the strength she could command. There was a shriek, and all the lights went out.

'Hes,' said Fanny gently, into the darkness, 'I think we should be trying to get out of here, don't you?'

They had crept a little way up the tunnel, to get away from that terrible room, but then their legs had given way under them, and they had fainted, more or less. Now they were sitting in the pitchest of dark, with their arms round each other, alone, it seemed, in the core of Bieldlaw.

Hester began to cry.

'We can't get out,' she sobbed. 'Oh, Fanny, we must be miles away from that door on to the hillside, and didn't you see how the passages twisted, and had openings out of them? And now it's dark. We could never find our way out. We'll wander round and round in here till we die.'

But Fanny said, 'No. I don't think so. As I came, I recognised the way. It's the maze, you see. These tunnels are the real maze, and the other things – the pendant, and the scratching on the hearth, and a stone I found in the garden – these were maps, if you like. But I don't need a map, Hes. I know the maze back to front and inside out. So if you'll stop crying, and hold my hand, I think I can get us out.'

Hester did not know what she was talking about, but Fanny's voice soothed her. So they stood up, and held hands tightly, and set off.

It is very difficult for the sighted to walk as if they were blind, never trusting the next step, straining their eyes into a blackness where no one could possibly see. It took hours for the two girls to tread the maze, with Hester clinging to her sister as Fanny ran her fingers lightly along the walls, finding gaps, groping for the wall again. Out of compassion each for the other, neither asked aloud the tormenting questions, Will the door still be open? How long have we been away? Fanny at least knew the theory that the supernatural time scale is different from that of the natural world. It was a sickening thought.

But her knowledge of the maze, at least, was true. After long creeping through the darkness, the girls saw ahead of them a tiny patch of lighter hue; as they moved towards it, it grew larger, and at last they emerged onto the hillside, under a navy blue sky pierced by glittering stars. It seemed radiance, after the blackness within.

'Hester,' Fanny said, 'do you want to rest, or shall we try to make it home?'

'Try to make it home,' said Hester in her normal voice. 'I don't fancy hanging about here, and the poor things will be frantic.'

Fanny hoped silently that the poor things were there to be frantic.

'Right,' she said.

So they went on down the slope, thankfully taking in gulps of the fresh night air. Far below them, they could now see the lights of the houses in Birkenshaw Gardens, and outside one of them – yes, their own – a car standing in the road with its lights on, and a blue lamp flashing on its roof.

'There's a Police car,' said Fanny, and tears came into her eyes for the first time. 'They're looking for us. It's still now.'

'Yes. It's over now,' Hester replied.

She was tireder than she had ever been in her life before, and thought that she could sleep, and sleep, and sleep.

But it was not over yet.

On the way down, neither girl had wanted to look back, up to the hateful summit of the hill. But as they got to the flat, grassy place where the standing stones were, and stopped to rest a moment, Hester cast a hasty glance over her shoulder, then turned right round, her eyes widening with astonishment and fear.

'Look, Fan,' she whispered in an awed voice.

Fanny turned too, and saw that the ring of trees was on fire. It had never been beautiful till now. Rising from the roots, red and yellow flames licked hungrily up every trunk, brushing the branches and setting light to the leaves, which burst like golden flowers into falling, glittering sparks.

'A volcano,' said Fanny wonderingly, then, in the instant that the earth cracked, 'Quick, Hes, quick!'

She threw herself down into the shelter of the standing stones, pulling Hester with her, not a moment too soon. With a noise that seemed to shatter the sky, Bieldlaw split down its length in a line of fire, and into the fissure fell the burning trees, and half the hillside. A terrible rumbling and crashing came from deep below the earth, and in the silence that followed it, Fanny heard weeping and moaning dying away upon the air.

Hester was lying flat on her face, crying, 'Oh, Mother, oh, Stuart! Oh, Mother!'

Fanny felt herself cautiously for injuries, and decided that she was unscathed. For the first time, she felt like giving Hester a hard kick.

'Shut up,' she said crisply. 'Are you hurt?'

'I don't think so,' Hester sniffed.

'Then let's go home.'

There were people running and shouting in the street, doors banging and sirens wailing, as they went down over the blackened grass towards Dr Mowbray, who had seen them, and was coming up to meet them.